Bain of my L

A Written History of W

.

Early this morning I was awoken by the

sound of a collared dove cooing to the world that his loved
one had been taken in the night by a cat. Well I'm guessing
that was what all the cooing was about, because a quick
glance out of the window as I made my ritual early
morning dash to the bathroom showed me that he was all
on his own. No sign of his wife at all. To be honest I don't
know if it was the boy or the girl dove that had been taken.
They both look identical to me. Maybe they were both
boys. A couple of gay doves. Or both girls. Lesbian doves.
 I'll stop there I think. I have no wish to be accused of
being judgemental. If I'm going to be totally honest in
these blogs (I don't think so) I must tell you, that I don't
even know if it was taken by a cat. Could have been
anything, an Owl for instance or, I'm just trying to think
what else could pluck a collared dove from a high tree at
night in total darkness. Maybe another Owl. I don't know.
 Maybe it didn't get taken at all. Perhaps it just got fed up
and pissed off. Probably been planning it for ages and
while its partner was sleeping, sloped off quietly to meet
its lover. It would have had to walk though, for fear that
the sound of its flapping wings would wake the other one
up. Well anyway the upshot was, that the betrayed partner
was very upset and the bloody thing woke me up with its
cooing. So, I shot it! Thereby putting us both out of our
misery. Those last two sentences are a total fabrication.
This little patch of mine is a wildlife sanctuary and no

were hurt during the making of this whole ‚h. But if it does it again tomorrow morning...

Whilst I'm about early morning rising, my cock has been causing me a few problems in the mornings as well. It's been an ongoing problem for some time now. It's quite a big old thing and can be a flipping nuisance. Especially when it crows right outside my bedroom window. I really like my old cock though and wouldn't want to be without it. I just hope the neighbours don't complain that's all. It can't help it. It's just doing what nature intended. It has always had a mind of its own. I call him "Wing Commander". I call him that because he's got wings and he is quite a commanding character. Also, because that's his name.

Right. Well that's it then. I'm off to bed. It's been a long day. Oh, and just before I go. Anything you might have read into the last paragraph is no fault of mine. It's your mind! Good night.

There are times when I get bored with low

fat spread on my toast and yearn for the full creamy taste of real butter. Yesterday morning was one such time and I thought to myself, "sod the cholesterol". Having made the momentous, and, if I say so myself, extremely brave decision. I am risking a heart attack here you know! I hurried down to the local shop. Where I purchased a nice slab of Lurpak. I was about to leave the shop when my eyes lit upon a new type of loaf. 'Our thickest slice ever', proclaimed the label, and just to hammer home the message a bit more, 'DOORSTEP'. "I'm having some of that", I quickly decided. Yes, I know, sometimes I can be completely reckless.

When I got home, I was almost drooling with anticipation. The thought of eating my thick doorsteps, with lashings of naughty butter dripping off hot toast was almost too much to bear.

Oh, bloody hell! Sorry, excuse my French. The bread was too thick to fit into the toaster! But do not despair. I was determined to have my hot buttered toast and managed after a bit of a struggle to force the slices in. Shouldn't have done that! Silly thing to do. I couldn't get them out! Stuck fast they were. Like a fat bloke in a turnstile.

Now please, please take good note. If ever you get your toast stuck in the toaster never try to get it out with a metal object. Such as a fork for example. It is extremely unwise. Especially if you forget to switch it off first!

Please don't be concerned. I am assured by the Paramedics that, after I recover from my slight concussion, I am going to be fine. Toaster is buggered though. Wasn't tough enough to withstand the explosion! Tomorrow, after the man from the electricity company has fitted the new fuse box, I shall buy a new toaster. One with wider openings. Well, I'm not going to waste all that lovely butter.

On my way into town today I was thinking how

quiet the roads are. Maybe it's got something to do with the price of petrol. Anyway, the road was remarkably clear and I was making good progress on my way to visit my friends Bob and Jackie. Who are, incidentally, lovely people. (I put that in just in case they read this). Blimey that sounds bad! No honest I mean this. They are lovely people.

Where was I? Oh yes. On my way to town. There was a car in front of me and I was gaining on it rapidly. It was moving very slowly, about twenty-five mph so I thought I would overtake it. Then suddenly had second thoughts about the overtaking and was stuck behind it for miles. No way was I going to overtake a 'Maserati'. I know what these drivers of powerful cars are like. Anyway, I don't like to race in my 'Nissan Serena'. I reckon I could have taken him though.

My Son George's phone has stopped

working. It's completely 'kaput'. This malfunction caused a bit of a crisis. When his Mother went to pick him up from college, she couldn't find him. After waiting twenty minutes or so and working herself up into a blue funk with worry, she called me. "I can't find George. Do you think he's alright?" I could hear the note of panic in her voice and tried to reassure her. "Don't be daft you silly cow". No I didn't really say that. I'm not that unfeeling. I just thought it. What I did say was. "What do you mean you can't find him? Where have you looked?"

Well it turns out she hadn't looked anywhere. She was sat in the car. I suggested, kindly, I thought, that if she was worried she should go to reception and see if they could help. On her way to the reception desk she 'found' George, who had no idea he was lost, sitting on a bench chatting to his mates, the way 17 year olds tend to do. Now don't tell her this, but I was a bit worried too. Well he is my boy. My little Georgie, my ickle bickle boy, my boysie woysie, my lickle....Sorry about that. Got carried away, a bit emotional.

There is a point to this little anecdote. It's this. If you want to keep in touch with someone, do not, I repeat, do not, put their mobile phone into the washing machine on a hot wash.

I bumped into a bloke down the

village today, outside the Co-op. Flipping expensive shop that. He greeted me heartily. "Hallo Dave, old mate. How you doing?" He carried on calling me Dave all through our conversation. Which just to let you know was about old bangers. When I say old banger, I'm talking about motors not some old tart! I realise that I should have pointed out his mistake to him sooner, but by the end of our conversation he almost had me convinced that my name was Dave. As we parted he said. "I'll pop in and see you sometime. You still living at...?" And he mentioned an address I'd never heard of let alone lived at. At this stage I realised that he didn't know me and I didn't know him. It's alright for him though. He thinks I'm Dave. I ain't got a bloody clue who he is!

I mentioned the other day

about the very early morning routine of the Wing Commander, my very handsome golden Cockerel. I am referring to him as a Cockerel from now on because some of you, I will mention no names here, seemed to get a bit over excited when I, in my total innocence, let me hasten to add, used the short and very proper old English word 'cock'.

What had been happening with the Wing Commander was that his internal clock had, for some reason unknown to me, become out of sync'. This had led to him rising very early in the mornings whilst it was still dark in fact, and proclaiming loudly, also very wrongly that it was dawn. When I say very early I am talking between one and two o'clock in the wee small hours. Really annoying. How I never got any complaints from the neighbours I just don't know.

But the problem has been solved. The wayward Cockerels clock has adjusted itself. I say the problem has been solved. What I should say, is that the problem has solved itself. Nature has come to the rescue, and indeed to the Wing Commanders rescue. Well, let's be honest here. He was in serious danger of having his neck stretched.

How has this miraculous inner clock adjustment been made? I shall tell you. Do you remember me telling you that two new young hens had arrived last week? Well it turns out that the Wing Commander has been tutoring his new young ladies in the arts of love. Sadly, I must inform you, that he has despoiled them both. He has acted like an utter cad. Their virtue is no more. Their cherries have been taken. In short and putting it bluntly. The Wing Commander has shagged them both! The ladies themselves are not without fault. After their initial reluctance, they are now willing partners in this debauchery. Giving themselves to him, without hesitation, in return for a worm or two. Of course, it should not be forgotten that the Wing Commander also has conjugal obligations to his other wives, and he does his utmost to fulfil those duties with vigour.

The result? Absolute blissful peace and quiet in the mornings. The Wing Commander has been having a bit of a lay in these last few mornings. Poor thing. He really is completely shagged out!

If there is such a thing as reincarnation I wouldn't mind coming back as a Cockerel. Better that, than being a complete and utter 'cock'!

Today I thought I'd pay a surprise visit to my friend

Glenn. I didn't phone him to let him know I was on my way, because usually when I do that he gets called out on some errand or other. It's uncanny the number of times that has happened in the past. I can't remember the number of times his old Granny has died, suddenly, just after I have phoned to say I'm on my way. Anyway, he was there today, and he did look pleasantly surprised to see me. Or maybe he just looked surprised, I don't really remember. It's been several hours since it happened, and I am getting on a bit now.

Glenn is the lead singer with the group 'Meander Lane'. A lot of people haven't heard of this group. Very many people. Lots and lots of people. A hell of a lot of people. Have you heard of them? No. I thought you wouldn't have done. I'm not surprised. Most of the population of the world haven't. But Glenn is a brilliant vocalist. He'll tell you that himself. Repeatedly. On and on, until you run away!

One of the best things about visiting Glenn is that he has his own 'state of the art' recording studio. If you are lucky you might not get invited to listen to his latest song. If you are unlucky you will have to endure, sorry did I say endure? I meant listen to. Did I say unlucky? Oh dear! I am a bit confused today. It's an age thing you know. What I'm trying to say is; he will invite you to 'have a listen'. It goes on and on for ages. You can't not listen because he always stands blocking the door. When the music stops, all you have to do, is tell him how good it sounds. You must tell him several times though, and he will eventually let you go.

He is an ex-soldier and used to work as a night club bouncer. Six foot six he stands on the ground and he weighs two hundred and thirty-five pounds. Hey! Didn't Johnny Cash used to sing that? But I think it is the fact that he is such a big bloke, which allows my mate Glenn to wear the kind of outfit he was wearing today. He's not that tough though. He was wearing a vest? His Mum makes him wear that. I think it makes him look a bit like Jeremy Clarkson's older sister?

Seriously though. Which I always am. Glenn is a smashing bloke. Straight as a die. He has women falling at his feet. I know this for a fact, because he has told me himself. Several times.

Just to finish off I mustn't forget to mention them again. 'Meander Lane' have just cut their first album. I was able to find it on Spotify by typing in the name. I'll say it again 'Meander Lane'. Go on. Google it. You know you want to.

It's no good I've got writer's cramp. Don't

know quite what to do about it. I have tried slapping myself around the face in the hope that something will loosen in my brain and allow me to carry on writing. So far it hasn't worked. Seems that my brain already has too many loose bits rattling around in there. Oops' hang on. Did I say writer's cramp? Sorry. I meant writers block!

The problem is that it has been a quiet kind of a day. Uneventful. Nothing to hang my hat on. I did get invited to dinner this evening by an old flame, but nothing happened there unfortunately. The meal was delicious though. Roast chicken with all the trimmings, followed by rhubarb and plum crumble with custard. But you don't want to hear about that, do you? No, I thought not.

I think what you are supposed to do in these circumstances is just to carry on writing any old nonsense. But that's not going to work, I write a lot of nonsense as it is. What I'm going to do is have another look in my notebook. See if I can find some inspiration there.

No, nothing there just random notes. Nothing happening in there to give my limited amount of grey matter a bit of a kick-start. Hold on a minute! I think we're off!

When I was a youngster I was the proud owner of a Triumph Tiger Cub motorbike. It was completely unreliable and often used to let me down just when I needed it most. In fact, it could be described as reliably unreliable. This little motorbike was at its most unreliable, at those times, when I had somehow persuaded one of the young ladies of the village, we called them young ladies in those days. They had to behave like ladies. The pill hadn't been invented yet! To join me for a romantic trip into the surrounding countryside. "I'll be there" I would promise in a foolhardy manner, adding hopefully. "Don't forget to bring a blanket".

Of course, knowing what a pig it was to get started I would allow myself plenty of time to accomplish this. Now this is the bit where I begin to tell you about the Tiger Cubs kick-start pedal. The bit which has been inspired by me using the word kick-start towards the end of the third paragraph. Clever eh!

The kick-start pedal frightened me! It frightened me because I knew that it could kick back violently. It was devious too and would often lull me into a false sense of security by starting on the first attempt. As soon as I heard it fire up I would turn the twistgrip frantically, revving the engine madly, desperately hoping that it would warm up and keeping running. My hopes building, rev rev, building rev rev dwindling rev gone. Phut!

Another half hour or so of fruitless painful attempts at kick-starting her -it had to be a her - and I would give up in despair. No romantic trip, no young lady, no blanket on the ground. Just two very painful ankles and bruised shins. Both ankles and both shins because I didn't give in easily. When one leg was knackered I would switch to the other one.

But I tell you what. I loved that little motor bike. I loved how she looked and I loved how she smelled, and when she did go, I loved how she went. No need for crash helmets in those days. You could feel the wind on your face and in your hair. The miles I rode her were worth all the miles I had to push her home. They were great days.

Just to finish on this bit. If you ever get the chance to ride a Tiger Cub just remember, if it doesn't start, it will be either; you haven't turned the ignition key, or you have forgotten to turn the petrol on! That's a bit of advice that was hard learned and hard earned.

The young lady? She went off with my mate Spud. He had a Norton Commando!

Sadie is the German Shepherd who lives with me, here on my little

patch. No I haven't got any sheep! Sadie is a German Shepherd of the canine variety. Although if I am honest with you, I would not be too upset if a beautiful blonde haired German woman with plaited hair, turned up at the door, begging me to let her move in and take care of me. They usually have plaits, don't they? Well they do in my fantasies. I am joking here. I don't have fantasies about German women. OK, perhaps just this once.

I refer to Sadie as the German Shepherd, because I really don't like to just call her the dog. She deserves better than that! I find it a comfort to have her around. She looks after security around here and she does a good job of deterring any unwanted visitor. By unwanted visitor I am not talking about the Mother-in-Law. Oh,yes, I am! Wait a minute, I don't have a Mother-in -Law any more. That joke is void. I mean anyone who is skulking around trying to see if I have anything worth pinching. Might as well tell them right now. I haven't. As my friends (I do have a couple) will tell you, Sadie is not in the slightest bit aggressive once she has got to know them, and will allow them to come in without hindrance. But luckily for me, she does have a very loud bark and lets me know in good time if strangers are about.

Sadie is not a house dog. She lives outside where she has her own kennel or the choice of many sheds in which she is free to take up residence. She prefers her own kennel though because it is right outside the door and she can keep a close eye on me and prevent me sneaking out on my own. Some people think Sadie should live indoors with me, but this little wagon does not have the space for a German Shepherd. Unless of course, as already mentioned above, the German Shepherd was a blonde Fraulein of the two-legged human type. Under those circumstances, I am sure I could fit her in somewhere.

Anyway, as I was saying, Sadie lives outside and it is a good job that she does. Unwanted visitors do not only come in human form. The local foxes are extremely partial to a chicken takeaway and are regular visitors. She is excellent at making them feel that her patch is not a good place to be. Also, Sadie does not like Magpies or Crows, and will not tolerate their presence. She must instinctively know that they steal eggs and kill and eat young chicks. Strangely enough, she never chases Lucky. Lucky is the tame Crow who was raised by my Son, and who has decided that she likes it here so much, that she is never going to leave. I will tell you the story of Lucky the Crow another time.

The reason I am talking about Sadie here, is that something crossed my mind today. The something is this. How is it that Sadie, who as I say is an outside dog, and has her own kennel? How is it, that, whenever I decide that I shall go and have a bit of a rest? A sit down and a read of the newspaper. How is it that Sadie is always sitting in my favourite chair?

Bigotry and prejudice. I am guilty of

both these things on occasion but I always do my best to keep such things in check. Because I am aware that they are wrong. Of course, they are. I hate the term political correctness but I suppose it does have its uses. Especially if it causes you to stop and think. It certainly thrives on issues such as these. Indeed, in today's world political correctness just thrives. But, and yes, I do know it's politically incorrect to say so, sometimes bigotry and prejudice can make me smile and even laugh out loud.

Take today for example. Sadie the German Shepherd and I decided we would take a walk to work up an appetite for lunch. When I say that we decided, I suppose what I really mean is that I decided. Whoever heard of a dog making a decision on whether we go for a walk or not? No. Hang on a minute! It was Sadie that decided on the walk. The more I think about it the clearer it becomes to me. Yes, it was Sadie. What happens is that she takes to following me like a shadow. Whenever I move she is there, getting under my feet and sometimes even causing me to stumble. Even actually tripping me on occasion. But it's the eyes that really get to me. Great big soulful eyes, looking up at me, or down if I've fallen over. Sad eyes imploring me to take pity on her and take her for a walk. I give in, I always do, and she knows even before I utter the words, "let's go for a walk", that I have given in to her. Off she goes, frolicking and vocalising in the way that German Shepherds do when they have browbeaten you into submission and bent you to their will. So, I will amend what I said before, and state categorically that Sadie decides. Now then, where was I before getting side-tracked? Oh yeah! Bigotry and prejudice made me laugh today. Perhaps it shouldn't have, but I'm afraid it did.

The smell of chips is sometimes hard to resist and today my resistance was low enough that I found myself buying a bag. A large bag that I would be able to share with Sadie. I know I shouldn't share with her but it's her eyes you know. Those big soulful eyes... Hold on, I'm not going there again.

We sat at a park bench, alongside an elderly chap who had the same idea as me and was eating a bag of chips.

"Alsatian", he said suddenly, pointing at Sadie. I wasn't sure whether he was asking me or telling me.

"Yeah". I said, "German Shepherd".

"No", he said. "That is an Alsatian".

I tried to put him right. "They used to be called Alsatians, now they are called German Shepherds".

" Yeah still an Alsatian though. Vicious bastard's I 'ate em, I 'ate all bleeding Germans".

I rose to my best friend's defence. "She wouldn't hurt a fly", I protested, momentarily forgetting Sadie's hatred of wasps, bees, and bluebottles. I gave her another chip to distract her in case she wanted to rip his throat out.

He wasn't finished. "I seen a programme about 'em. They was training 'em to be vicious. It was on tele. What was it called"? He asked himself. "Sumfing abart dogs. What was it"? He looked at me quizzically.

"I don't know. I don't watch a lot of television". I answered, lying through my teeth. I had gone off him.

"You don't watch tele". He was sneering. "You don't watch tele?" He turned it into a question.

"I said I don't watch a lot of television. I like to watch wildlife programmes and I like quizzes". I really disliked him now.

"Countdown. Do you like countdown"?

"I used to like it. I've gone off it a bit now."

"Yeah. I bet you went off it when Carol left didn't ya? She's got a lovely arse, ain't she?" I never answered him. I didn't like to admit he was right. On both counts. "What's your favourite thing on tele?" He asked.

I swallowed a mouthful of chips before answering. "I like Stephen Fry. Anything with Stephen Fry in it."

"Stephen Fry! Stephen Fry! He's a bleeding poof!"

"Yeah he is Gay". I said, adding. "but he's none practicing".

"None practicing! None practicing!" He was indignant. "'E don't need to bloody practice. 'E's been at it for years! 'Ear you're not a gay boy are ya?"

Sadie and me, having finished our chips, got up and went on our way. Hopefully leaving the miserable old git wondering what it was I found so funny.

So, there you have it. Prejudice, sexism and bigotry, all in one short conversation. Political correctness. It doesn't always get its message across. You've got to laugh!

Weather-wise it has been a beautiful, warm, sunny day. It's not even summer yet but the temperature must have been up in the seventies. It gets us British folk up and about doesn't it? We love to make the most of these first warm days. Get out in the sun. Absolute bliss. Get the sun lounger out, and settle back. Maybe have a book with you, in case you can summon up enough strength to turn a few pages. Have a bit of a read? Lovely stuff. Why not doze off for a bit? Have a bit of a kip? Go on. Why not?

Why not, why not? I'll tell you why not. Lawn mowers. That's why not. First bit of decent sunny weather and out they come, to irritate and annoy. Screeching, whining, buzzing and incessant lawn mowers. Loud lawn mowers, irritating switch on switch off electric lawn mowers, strimmer's, brush cutters, chainsaws, hedge trimmers and leaf blowers. That's why flipping not!

It is difficult if not impossible, to get away from the noise we all seem so intent on making. Even in the so-called dead of night there will be someone or something intent on disturbing the peace. There is always the distant drone of moving traffic. Be it road, rail, air or sea. Here it is now, just after midnight and a motorcyclist has decided to take advantage of the relatively empty roads and go for a high-speed tear up. Ripping past the houses full of sleeping humanity, with a complete disregard for their need of a peaceful night's sleep. A couple of goods trains have just sauntered past. On their way to who knows where. Strangely enough the sound of a train at night, is to me a comforting one. Can't imagine why that should be. Nothing primordial about trains. So, it can't hark back to a basic instinct. Can it? Difficult one to work out. Don't think I will bother.

Sometimes I like to imagine how quiet life was before the invention of the infernal combustion engine or the electric motor. I said infernal combustion engine just then. It wasn't a slip of the pen. But quietness is something it is very hard to imagine. Besides I have an awful feeling that perhaps complete and utter silence would drive us all crazy. After all isn't sound deprivation used as a form of torture?

I imagine that the towns and cities of the old days were quite noisy places. Where even the hustle and bustle of everyday life could generate quite a bit of noise. But in the countryside, surely it must have been blissfully quiet. Nothing to disturb the peace except birdsong and the occasional lowing of cattle or bleating of sheep. Truth is if course, that we will never know.

Oh well, back to reality and the cacophony of sound that is our modern life. It might not be the peace and quiet we hoped for when we unfolded the sun lounger, but at least the sun is warm on our pale, light deprived bodies. So,let's ignore the noise as best we can and have a nice little forty winks.

Oh, for heaven's sake! Who's lit that bloody bonfire?

Mirrors! I don't like 'em. They always tell the most awful, painful and obviously blatant lies. Whenever I look into a mirror, I see this really ancient and decrepit old bloke looking back at me. Wrinkled as an old walnut and hairier than a bill posters glue brush.

These ugly features taunt me mercilessly. "Who are you looking for John? Who did you expect to see? Don't tell me you expected to see a young John. Well I've got news for you mate. He is gone, and he ain't never coming back. In fact, I have to tell you, things are only going to get worse"!

It's not a lie, though is it? It's the plain, simple and sadly unvarnished truth. I'm not going to come back. The young, and dare I say it, handsome young John, has gone forever. Replaced by a rough and ever increasingly baggier and saggier old man. There is nothing to be done. It must be accepted, because it is the inevitable consequence of getting old. Of course, some people, those with perhaps more money than sense, resort to plastic surgery in an effort to stave off the ravages of time. That is not for me though, and not just because I don't have the money. From what I have seen of those who do take the surgery option, it just doesn't work. They tend to end up looking like grotesque parodies of their former selves.

I suppose one option open to me is to avoid mirrors but that is easier said than done. Besides, there are always other ways that you can be caught out. Shop windows for example. I keep on getting unexpected and unpleasant glimpses of the truth as I pass by. Also, in nearly every shop you go into these days there are the ubiquitous closed circuit TV cameras, with their nosy little lenses attempting to pry into our every little unguarded moment. They have the cheek to ask us to smile because we are on camera. Well I don't want to smile thank you very much. Smiling just makes me look worse than ever. Anyway, I find it hard to smile when I am concentrating on trying to remember not to scratch my backside, or pick my nose. Because I know some pimply youth in a back room somewhere is watching my every move.

Now just suppose that I was looking for a woman to share my life with. The thought does occasionally pass through my mind. Usually when I am looking at a pile of washing up or notice the build-up of dust on various shelves about the place. Well, how am I to meet the woman of my yearning dreams? The answer is of course that I am not. Unless I join a dating agency that caters for sad old men. Not that I would join such an agency. I have my pride you know. But let us suppose, purely for the purpose of writing this article, that I have joined such an agency, and I must write an honest description. It would have to go like this. Short, fat, balding, old bloke, with fading eyesight, rheumatic joints and no money would like to meet...

Hopeless, isn't it? What chance have I got? None.

So here is what I intend to do. Try extra hard in future to avoid mirrors and all those other niggling, everyday reminders of my inevitable decline, and concentrate instead, on the fact that I have been blessed with a fantastic libido, yes ladies it's true, and that I am still, in my imagination, possessed of the good looks of my youth.

In conclusion. I would like to point out, that the chauvinistic remarks, about washing up and dusting, which I referred to earlier, are only there for comic effect. They in no way reflect my true thoughts on the role of women in society. But if anyone is interested...

This morning quite early I was

standing before the toilet bowl. I don't remember why. Oh yes, that's it, I was having a pee! Anyway, that's not important. I say that's not important, but when you get to my age, it does take on a greater importance than it used to in my youth. Well, for a start, you must stand there a lot longer just waiting for things to happen. Even if you are almost bursting it seems that nature likes to play its little jokes on us older folk and restrict the flow until the pain is almost, but not quite, unbearable. Then a bit of relief, then a break, then a bit more relief. The whole rigmarole takes ages and on a cold morning is not even slightly amusing. Although I will admit that it might amuse any onlookers. Not that I have any onlookers. Of course, when I was a boy there were onlookers. Me and my mates used to have competitions to see who could pee the highest. I am proud to say that I did win occasionally. Today? I doubt if I could win a dribbling contest! But hey! Enough! Let me move on from this unsavoury subject.

As I was saying before I went off on my revelry. As I stood there beside the porcelain borehole, I noticed an earwig trying to clamber from the water and attempt to scale the slippery side of the bowl. He was of course unsuccessful. I'm sure me giving him an extra little sprinkling didn't help either, and after observing his valiant efforts for a minute or two, I flushed the toilet and watched him spiral to his death. After washing my hands, which apparently one should always do after using the facilities, I left the bathroom and decided to have some breakfast.

The guilt set in as I waited for the toast to burn. Why did I flush the earwig away? Why did that poor earwig have to die? If it had been a butterfly struggling in the water I would have rescued it, or a ladybird, or a bumble bee, or even a spider. There is no doubt that I would have come to its aid. No doubt at all.

I am ashamed of myself. I will tell you why as I dry my tears, and scrape the carbon from my toast.

That earwig had to die, because, and here I try to hold back my self-loathing. It had to die because it was ugly! There! I've said it! I have admitted here in black and white -all right then, brown and white- that I make decisions, based on looks. Not just on insects either. I do it with people too. Good job the toilet isn't a bit bigger. I might be tempted to flush away a few. But wait! Isn't that true of us all? Or at least a whole lot of us. Aren't most of us guilty of being judgemental about appearances sometimes? Who would you be attracted to first? Would it be the person with the happy smiling open countenance, or the surly downcast looks of another? Human nature provides the answer. We cannot help but respond to the happy smile and we instinctively neglect the frown. But we do this at our peril, and should remember that the evil assassin easily hides his true intent with a smile.

That earwig has given me food for thought. From this day on, I shall take time to get to know those who may not conform to the "norm". I will base my opinions, not on the shape of a person's face or the contours of their body, but on the content of their heart. Or at least I will try to. Can't really do better than that. I am only human after all is said and done.

Did you know that the earwig is a very beneficial insect to have in the garden? It's true. Go and google earwig. You'll be impressed.

Now if you will excuse me, I must go and inspect the manhole. With a bit of luck, that earwig might have managed to hang on to something. I may be able to save him. Give him a hot bath and a bit of burnt toast. Who knows we might even become good friends. Unlikely though, no one likes to be pissed on. That is unforgiveable.

His given name was Robert Ferguson. I

knew him as "Fergie" and his friends called him "Barney". My Mother who knew him more intimately than most, if you get my drift, very often referred to him as "that drunken bastard". She meant it too on occasions, but there was something between them. Something that kept them tied to each other, through thick and thin. Even though my Mum married many times, Fergie was always there in the background.

The first time I met Fergie was when I was about four or five years old. So, it would have been the early 50's. At that time, I was a resident of Shirley Residential Children's Home just outside Croydon in Surrey - later renamed "Shirley Oaks"- and Mum introduced him to me, on one of her rare -becoming increasingly more rare- visits.

Even though I was very young, I can remember the meeting very clearly. Fergie was a big man. He had a sagging lower lip which had the ability to retain a soggy roll up fag without any help from the upper lip. His nose was enormous and flattened across his face. Looking back on that meeting now I think that he must have known me before, because he scooped me up in his arms, hugged me and planted a wet kiss on my cheek. He had a few days' growth of bristle and it was unpleasantly sharp on my face. In subsequent meetings over the years I never remember him being clean shaven. Today I suppose it would be fashionable, and called designer stubble, but Fergie's face, was far too marked by life and excess to be fashionable. He smelled strongly of alcohol and tobacco. A smell I was to become familiar with over the years and something which I cannot remember as being unpleasant. Rather the reverse in fact.

The rest of that first meeting with him, was spent with me shyly peeking out at him from behind my Mothers coat. He had three fingers missing from his right hand -a sawmill accident- and a very big gold ear ring in his left ear lobe. Up until then I had thought that only villains in Enid Blyton books had ear rings, so my observations of this big man were somewhat tinged with fear. Later I learned that Fergie was a man to be wary of. But not by me, or anyone that he loved.

Mum and Fergie vanished from my life for several years after that and I was an unhappy child for a lot of the time. I suppose the authorities did their best for me. I remember different foster parents and foster aunts and uncles, and I suppose I was happy sometimes. But you know, a child needs a Mother, no matter how feckless she might be. I longed for her return.

She appeared back into my life as suddenly and as unexpectedly as she had left it. I was twelve years old and living with foster parents in London.

I hadn't seen her for six or seven years, and there she was! Not quite the beautiful princess of my imagination, but there she was, my beautiful, sweet faced Mum.

Everything happened so fast then. My clothes were flung into a suitcase. I hardly had time to say goodbye. It was into the waiting black taxi and off we went.

I had been unhappy most of the time in that particular foster home. The foster mum was a nasty and abusive woman given to handing out regular beatings and her son was a bully who obviously resented my presence, and made my life hell. But I was very fond of the foster Dad, a kindly, and caring man, who was obviously fond of me in return. That was my only regret at leaving. Not being able to say goodbye to him. Maybe though that was just as well. It would have been difficult for us both.

So, there I was at Victoria station, on board the famous "Flying Scotsman". On my way to a new and hopefully happier life. It is so difficult to describe my emotions on that momentous day. But have a try at imagining yourself as a child, thinking yourself abandoned forever. Then suddenly, there you are. Back in the arms of your Mother. I can tell you I was bewildered. Bewildered but happy.

This was the time when I properly got to know Fergie. Trawlerman, lumberjack, saw doctor, and cook. Fergie the fighter, the binge drinker, the bad man and the good man. Often down, Often down and out. But always there for me, when I had nowhere else to go.

He has gone now. Been dead for many a long year, but hardly a day goes by when I don't think of him.

It is quite amazing, the number of

women out there in small ad lonely heart land. A heck of a lot of them list among their interests, theatre, travel and dining out.

Come on now ladies. You are advertising in the free ads. Be honest. When did you last dine out and go to the theatre? Let alone take a flight to gay Paree to do so. I think, and I admit that I am no expert in these matters, but I think what you really mean is, that, theatre, travel, and dining out are the things you dream about doing when Mr Perfect, also known as Mr Right comes along. Well I'm sorry about this, but it has to be said. If he is out there, this perfect man. It is an almost odds on racing certainty that he has already been spoken for. There is no way that Mr Perfect or Mr Right, if indeed such a man exists, is sitting at home alone, in his wood panel lined study, in his grand mansion house, thinking despondently to himself. 'She must be out there somewhere, the woman of my dreams. She must be'. As he sobs, and flicks wistfully through the lonely heart ads, in the free local newspaper, which is pushed through his ornate brass letter box, every Wednesday morning.

Sad as I am to say it ladies. Maybe it is time to think again. Perhaps lower your sights just a little. Why not look for an ordinary bloke? The type of man who is happy to go out to work every day. Who brings home an average working man's wage. The kind of man who, although he can't afford to wine and dine you every day, and most definitely can't afford to take you to exotic destinations, nevertheless, loves you, and treats you with the respect you deserve.

What's that you say? He sounds a lot like the boring bloke you just divorced. Oh dear! That is bad news. Because he is exactly the same person that is reading your lonely heart ad right now. It could be your ex-husband, sitting in his lonely bedsit. Which is all the poor devil can afford these days. Eating a can of beans which he has tried to heat, unsuccessfully, on a warm radiator, who is reading your ad and trying to pluck up the courage to call your box number. Doesn't your heart just bleed for him? He is probably thinking about taking out a bank loan so that he can fulfil your wishes, and meet your criteria to be wined and dined.

You are thinking such a thing is unlikely to happen. Your ex-husband answering your lonely heart appeal. Well yes, it does sound unlikely. But it is not impossible. I know a couple who it happened to. I won't give their names so as not to embarrass them. Roger and Jill. They did meet up in these same circumstances. They fell in love all over again and remarried. At first, they would go out every week for a meal in a nice restaurant. But she got bored with that. So now they just have the occasional night out and a holiday abroad a couple of times a year. They are very happy.

You may be wondering, what I am doing, looking through the lonely-hearts adverts? Am I lonely? Am I, as it says in the ads, looking for companionship, maybe more? Has my eye been caught by tall, leggy lady, curvy, caring and genuine, solvent with own home?

Well, perhaps I do get a little lonely sometimes. Yearn for some feminine comfort. But the truth is, I was just idly glancing through the ads as I ate my burnt toast this morning. No seriously I was. Oh, all right then, I'll admit it. I wasn't just glancing through. I was looking for a woman. There! Happy now? Luckily for me I soon came to my senses and got a grip of myself. No! Not like that. For heaven's sake! Anyway, it got me thinking, and this little article is the result of those thoughts. But, the fact is, that even if I were seriously seeking a mate, I have grave doubts as to whether I could meet the criteria demanded by some of these ladies.

Take this one for example: Voluptuous attractive tanned, well-groomed blonde, looking for good times, seeks tall, well-built guy, for pampering, massages and discreet friendship. Any age/looks.

That rules me right out. How can I be discreet? I need stuff to put in my blog. Besides which, I have my suspicions that the word voluptuous could be a euphemism for, 'extremely large'.

Don't worry it isn't just your fault. I blame the

government for all our woes. The government and the bloody supermarkets. Well, someone must take the blame, and it ain't going to be me. Although I have deprived the government of some revenue, by giving up smoking. I'm sorry about that, but I thought I would try and gain a few more years of not breathing through a piece of plastic tubing.

I am drifting right away from the point of this item. I wanted to share with you my sadness at what looks likely to be the end of the British pub as we know and love it. But also, and very importantly. What is to become of that other great British tradition, the pub character, the bar stool eccentric? Someone like Norman, for instance.

Norman belongs to that fairly ubiquitous type of bar stool drunk. The kind that likes to regale the hapless pub goer with imagined stories of their heroism in the field of conflict. The pseudo SAS soldier. Usually they are tolerated for what they are, bullshitters, and become the butt of the pub comedian's jokes. The pub comedian incidentally, is not usually very funny. But his alcohol intake gives him the confidence to tell his, usually racist jokes with impunity. He thinks people are laughing at his wit, when in reality they are laughing about him.

Norman was different from the usual bar stool soldier, in that he was not a braggart. At least not in the sense of the normal pub boaster. Norman thrived on keeping his imaginings close to his chest. He liked to draw the unwary listener close. Norman liked to reveal his SAS secrets very quietly. Those of us in the know, referred to Norman as 'the whispering soldier'.

"Good evening Landlord," said the thirsty stranger. "A pint of your finest ale. If I may." He didn't really say this. but I thought it gave better dramatic effect. He probably just said. "Pint of bitter please mate."

While the stranger supped his pint, Norman will have been observing him surreptitiously for a few minutes. Before moving in for the kill.

"Hunc mmmnum," Norman would mumble. "Hnnn na mmmnn."

"Sorry mate, what was that?"

"Nnnnam em nannam Korea war."

"Oh, right Korean war, Yeah."

"fiddy fo serrrrnn SAS."

"SAS, you were SAS?"

Hearing this loud utterance Norman would glance quickly and furtively over his shoulder, and put a cautionarybony finger to his lips, before raising his pint glass and noticing theatrically that it was empty.

At this point the stranger would invariably ask. "Fancy another?"

Normans glass was in the Landlords hand, and the pump handle already in a downward trajectory, almost but not quite, before the question had been asked. Honed by years of practice, Normans free drink routine was masterful, and almost never failed.

"Mumble mutter mumble," Norman would whisper, as his victim strained to listen.

"Mumble middle east. Desert."

"Arabs, mumble sand dune."

"Rifle mumble took 'is 'ed off. Mumble whisper."

"All mumble mutter kill mutter mutter."

"Machine gun, whisper mutter mumble."

"Dead mumble, all of 'em whisper."

After several ear straining minutes of this the stranger would gulp his beer down, say an urgent goodbye and head swiftly for the exit.

This moment was the only time anyone ever heard Norman raise his voice above a whisper.

"You never heard it from me!" He would exclaim loudly, sitting bolt upright and squaring his thin shoulders. "Official secrets act. I never said nothin'."

At that he would slump back into his bar stool, a quiet satisfied smile playing on his lips.

If the pub does disappear, where will Norman and his like go? Where will they find an outlet for their eccentricities? I tell you, it's never going to be the same. Why do we let these things happen? Why?

When I was a very small boy I loved to listen to the songs of the day. Did we have a hit parade in those days? I'm not sure, but I think we did. This is the early 1950's I'm talking about. Connie Francis springs to mind, Alma Cogan, Frankie Laine. Oh yes, of course, mustn't forget Doris Day! She was so pretty. I think I fell in love with Doris when I was about six years old.

I must have been a bit of a precocious child, because I was also madly besotted with one of my teachers, the wonderful, beautifully fragrant, Mrs Williams. She of the fluffy woollen jumpers. Is it angora? I can remember the feeling that I wanted to snuggle into her ample cuddleness. I just made up that last word, but it fits the bill nicely. Oh, Mrs Williams, if you knew how this small boy felt when you stood close to him in class. I am sure you would blush with embarrassment. Six years old! Crikey!

In truth, I know what it was. I needed a Mothers love, and my real Mum not being there, any woman showing the slightest maternal kindness, became the target of my ardent attentions. That's my excuse anyway!

Here I go again, getting distracted from what I wanted to talk about. Now where was I? Yes music. That's today's theme.

The radio was piped into the children's room from the staff room, which was at the other end of the house. If we kids were playing indoors, it must have been raining or bitterly cold outside. Or perhaps it was early evening. But anyway, we were enjoying the privilege of listening to the radio. Obviously, none of us had misbehaved that day. I became aware of a song playing. It was called 'Scarlet Ribbons', and it was sung movingly by the mellifluous voiced Mr Harry Belafonte. I loved it!

What a man. He had gone out at Christmas looking for ribbons for his daughter's hair. An impossible task. All the shops were closed and shuttered. All the streets were cold and bare.

Well what happened was, when he returned home, empty handed and very sad. He discovered that there were scarlet ribbons on her bed. He thought it was a miracle from God, and sang this lovely song about it. At the time being only six years old I went along with the miracle bit. Now that I am older and wiser I have reached the conclusion that his wife put the ribbons there, and that Harry was a bit too stupid or maybe had imbibed too liberally of Christmas liquor to realise that. But anyway, at the time I gave him the benefit of the doubt, and I loved the song. I wanted the record.

Again here, I think perhaps not having a Father of my own, I have latched on to Mr Belafonte's fatherly concern for his child's happiness, and decided that he is the one for me. What a complex child I must have been, and probably irritated the hell out of people with my neediness. I haven't changed much!

My pocket money, as decreed by the London County Council, was three pennies a week. Thrupence we called it. We kids would be taken to the local sweet shop (just outside the homes gates) where we would indulge our urgent need for tooth decay. Probably, I would get one gobstopper for a penny, and half a dozen blackjacks and the money was gone.

However, I wanted to buy that record which was priced at two shillings and sixpence. An absolute fortune! I began to save my pocket money every week. Actually, the powers that be, saved it for me. Even so, it was very difficult watching the other kids get their sweets each week. Especially as I still had to go to the shops with them. Children's homes routines must not be broken.

It's taken me a while but I have managed to work out that it took me six, no, seven, wait a bit. Yes, it took me eight... erm, ten weeks to save the money.

We went on the bus, the assistant house mother and I, to nearby Croydon. Where finally I could buy, 'Scarlet Ribbons' by Mr Harry Belafonte.

What excitement there was back at the home. The record player was situated in the staff room, and all the kids were summoned to the staff room door to listen as my longed for, and hard won record, was played.

How proud I was, that this shiny piece of plastic was mine. I listened intently to each and every word.

Afterwards because it might get damaged, the record was put into the cupboard for safe keeping.

I never saw or heard that record again! Ten weeks without sweets. Ten weeks! Played once! Well a valuable lesson learned I think.

Shortly after this I heard Max Bygraves singing 'Tulips from Amsterdam'. Oh no! Not again!

As a portrait artist, I have, over the

years, had the great privilege, to paint and draw the features of many people. Making peoples portraits is something I really enjoy. I must make a living at it, so of course, I have to charge a fee for my time and endeavour. However, there are some portraits I will gladly do without charge, purely for the pleasure of it. Sometimes a beautiful child's face will catch my ever-searching eye, or it might be an elderly person with the wonderful wrinkles of time etched upon them. It could be the sharp angular shape of a nose or chin. It could be many things. But the thing about a person that is guaranteed to grab my attention and get my artistic juices flowing, is red hair. Commonly referred to as ginger hair.

Unfortunately to call someone 'ginger' is usually these days, in its mildest form teasing, and in its harshest form bullying.I am on the subject of ginger hair for a reason today.

A friend of mine has a daughter with beautiful hair, which is the colour of burnished copper. I say is, the colour of burnished copper. I should say was, the colour of burnished copper. It is now jet black.

Why has she dyed her lovely hair black? A colour which is totally unsuited to her complexion. The answer is, too many teasing comments, too many harsh remarks. It is bullying. Nasty, and thoughtless criticisms, with a total and reckless disregard, for a young girl's sensitivities.

It is not the done thing in these so called enlightened days to make cruel remarks about a person's race, colour, or creed. People with disabilities, or anyone who is slightly different to the so called 'norm', are no longer mocked as they sadly once were.

So why is it still alright for a person to be bullied because of the colour of their hair? I don't know the answer. What I do know, is that discrimination in any form is wrong. It should not be tolerated and society is rightly fighting against it, in all its forms.

Crikey! I think I'm making myself sound like a flipping saint. Sorry I don't mean to. I am as bad as many others, but the thing is, I do try to understand things, and if we all just tried to think a bit more, before we make our opinions known, then surely the world would be a better place.

The Oxford English dictionary describes 'ginger' as making something, or someone, more lively and exciting. I think they have got it right!

I have just noticed that all my pets are 'ginger'? Apart from 'Lucky' the crow, who would probably like to be, so that he could sneak in, and steal the hen's food without getting picked on.

Artists have always been drawn to the redhead. (Accidental pun there). The 16th century Venetian artist Titian, arguably the world's finest, was a prolific painter of ladies with red hair. Even lending his name to the genre. The reason being of course that he saw red hair, not as ginger, but for what it truly is. A natural palette of delicious warm colours. From deep burgundy, through to bright copper and orange.

Here is an admission. Well over forty years as an artist, and I have just had to look in the dictionary, for how to spell palette. Disgraceful!

The next time you have the pleasure of seeing, or being in the company of, someone you would normally describe as 'ginger', take a closer look. Perhaps offer them a compliment on it. You are in the presence of great beauty.

Just a thought to end on. If it happens to be a bloke, over six feet tall, and built like the proverbial brick outhouse, who has the red hair, it would perhaps be wise not to look too closely. Also, probably safer to forget the compliment. Anyway, you know what I mean.

Funny the things that can set me off at a tangent. No wonder I'm so hopeless at getting things done. Today my mission in life was to get my lawn mower working. I was out there in the shed fiddling about with spanners and screw drivers, pretending I knew what I was doing, when I really do not have a clue about things mechanical.

I have a comprehensive list of what could possibly be wrong with the lawnmower because I googled the not working symptoms and I now have an encyclopaedic knowledge of my particular make, the Countax K14. Unfortunately, even if I possessed a first-class honours degree in lawnmowing machinery from Oxbridge university I would still lack the mechanical skills to turn theory into fact.

So, I did what I usually do when I am stuck with a problem. I turned to Buddhist philosophy. The one I most like is this. If a problem can be solved it is not a problem, and if it can't be solved it is not worth worrying about. I decided to put aside my mechanical aspirations, and threw the spanners back into their box.

Now what to do next. Obviously, the grass wasn't going to get cut. But there is still the driveway to be tidied, and I need to make a nesting box for the broody hen. Sadie's kennel requires a bit of attention, and I must sort out the studio. There is still a lot of painting to be done on my wagon and... Oh, what the hell! Let's go for a nice walk.

It was still quite early, so not too hot, and the sun was warm and pleasant on my back. I called Sadie, the German Shepherd, who being the loyal and faithful hound that she is, was indoors sleeping on my favourite chair.

Our regular and familiar walk, is a circuitous route, part of which takes us through the local park. It was here that I noticed the elderly man sitting on a bench, smoking a pipe. He had removed his jacket and rolled up his shirt sleeves, and looked so relaxed, and delightfully old fashioned as he puffed away.

Seemingly lost in thought, he appeared to be unaware of our presence as we passed by. The scent of tobacco was wafted towards me and the pleasing aroma recalled memories of my childhood, when pipe smoking was a perfectly normal and acceptable practice.

It is a long time since I gave up smoking, but I remembered as we walked home, Sadie and I, that I had a pipe of my own somewhere in the back of a cupboard. I decided to look it out. Not to smoke of course, but just for the nostalgic pleasure.

Now look here, I may be getting on a bit, but sometimes I still get a childish pleasure out of things. Which is how I came to be posing in front of the mirror, pipe between my teeth, deciding what angle I looked best at. Yes indeed, after careful consideration, I have decided that my pipe lends me an air of intelligence. A contemplative sophistication. A look of distinction. In short, I think I look good with a pipe. What do you think?

Hmmm.. Perhaps I should take up smoking again? Can't quite make my mind up. Hmmm...

Thinking about it, I don't have to light it. Perhaps I'll just suck on it for a while, as I intelligently contemplate what to do about the damn lawnmower!

We all like to paint ourselves in a good light,

don't we? But if I'm to continue to use this blog as a cathartic exercise as well as entertaining people with a hopefully interesting read, then I must be truthful in what I write.

This is the reason I'm admitting today, that I was a horrible attention seeking little so and so when I was a teenager. A reaction perhaps to the fact that I didn't get a lot of attention -at least not of the positive kind- during my formative years.

My decline from a promising and somewhat placid child, albeit one with a temper apparently, to loud, rebellious teenager, started almost as soon as I began living with my Mother, after many years of being under the care of the London County Council children's department. Allowing me to live with my extremely volatile Mother, turned out to be a big mistake on the part of the authorities. But this is a part of my life which I will bore you with another time.

Going to school in Scotland was something I found very difficult. I found it difficult in England too if I'm honest about it. But in Scotland I had to contend with, not only the local dialect, but also the fact that I spoke with a broad London accent. Something which caused a lot of amusement to my peers, and which almost inevitably led to bullying from some of them.

Now I didn't spend years in children's homes and foster care, without learning how to take care of myself in these kind of circumstances, and I could quickly show these village school upstarts, exactly how a tough London kid could stick up for himself. Unfortunately, in doing so I gained a reputation. Not just amongst the kids but the teachers also.

The science teacher Mr Boswell didn't like me. He wasn't used to kids that talked back. I didn't like him either. So, in that respect we were on a fairly even level. However, Mr Boswell had somewhat of an advantage in our mutual hatred. Mr Boswell had the tawse. The tawse was the favoured method of corporal punishment in Scottish schools. It was a vicious two thonged hard leather strap. Usually applied to the palm of the hand, but sometimes, in the case of certain, to my mind, suspect teachers, the buttocks. It hurt like hell! Mr Boswell was fond of applying the tawse.

All right, I know that I should not have done it. But it should be borne in mind that I was a 13-year-old boy in the grip of some gruesomely nasty hormonal changesand carrying an enormous chip on my shoulder about the way life had treated me so far. Anyway, that apart, looking back on it now, even from an adult standpoint it seems a relatively minor misdemeanour.

What I had done was to make a poster during art class. Even though I do say so myself, it was a beautiful piece of artwork. I was proud of it. I thought I had got the colours spot on, and the lettering, which had taken some considerable time and diligence on my part, spelled out in large and beautifully constructed format the words, 'MR BOSWELL IS A BIG FAT BASTARD.

Not wanting to waste this magnificent piece of work, I waited until the class was empty and pinned it to the wall. Then went home for the weekend.

For some odd reason, I can recall the following Monday morning with great clarity. It began normally enough with a maths lesson, but it wasn't long before a strange thing started happening. One by one my classmates were called out of the room, only to return a few seconds later. This went on and on. Until there were just a few of us boys left. George went out, and returned seconds later. I looked at him. Was he avoiding my gaze? Gavin, my best friend, went out and duly returned a few seconds later. I was the only one left to go. I tried to get Gavin's attention but he was definitely not going to look at me. Of course, by this time I knew something was up. The whole class was quiet. Everyone had their head down, seemingly lost in concentration.

It was my turn and nervously curious I went into the classroom next door. The headmaster, or as he was known in the local dialect the 'Dominee', was standing there with my nemesis Mr Boswell. I also could not fail to notice that my colourful poster was pinned slap bang in the middle of the blackboard. The Dominee was wearing his black gown and mortarboard cap. They take education seriously in Scotland. It was a forbidding sight.

Now I ask you what was the point of such a long-protracted process? Why would two grown and supposedly intelligent men go through all this rigmarole? It was obviously my work. Look, there is my signature in the bottom right hand corner. Even today forty years later I am beginning to get my dander up. The only answer I can come up with is that they enjoyed the whole process. Hey! Who are the kids here?

Mr Boswell opened the desk drawer and took out the tawse. The usual punishment for misdemeanours was one stinging blow to each hand. On this occasion, he had other intentions. My hands and wrists -he wasn't very accurate- were subjected to six, increasingly painful blows. It was an excruciating punishment to inflict on anyone, let alone a child. Thank God that common sense finally prevailed and corporal punishment was abolished.

After I had numbed the pain somewhat under the cold tap, I returned to the classroom. It wasn't only my hands that hurt, it was my pride. How were my classmates to know that my tears were tears of rage and not because I wasn't tough enough to take the pain? I swore that when I grew up I would make Mr Boswell suffer.

That day at the age of 13 signalled the end of my school life. I hardly ever went back except when the school board forced me to. Although I was expected to do well, I never took any exams, and my leaving certificate may as well have been a blank piece of paper, for all it was worth.

All my own fault? Perhaps, but I was only a child and knew no better. We expect too much of kids sometimes. It is easy to forget that the young brain is still growing and needs time to mature.

 I would just like to finish by saying that I met Mr Boswell many years later. I felt no malice towards him. I had it seems, grown up.

Today if I were to make a poster about him, I would leave out the word fat. I think that was what upset him!

If I had a pound coin, for every time I
have heard a woman utter the phrase "Men! They're all the same", or variations on that theme, I would probably have very heavy pockets. Carrying all those coins around would very likely, make holes in my pockets. But that'll be no problem. I happen to know that women are very handy

with a needle and thread. What a thing to say! I don't know. Honestly us men, what are we like eh?

So many coins though. I'd be able to invite a woman out for a meal in a posh restaurant, with wine, and stuff. Like those fancy little flat after eight mints, they charge you a fortune for, just because they've got their own little envelope. Oh, and a finger bowl so that we could clean our fingers after the chocolates. Women love all that sort of thing. They love to be cared for like the delicate little flowers they are. Luckily us men always know how to treat our lady friends. Oops! Shouldn't have said that. Men! What are we like?

After the posh meal, she will no doubt be in a hurry to get you back to her place for "coffee". Yeah right! We know what "coffee" means, don't we guys? We know. Oh no! What am I saying? What am I like? Men!

It's only right though, don't you think? That a chap should get some reward, after treating her to such a romantic evening out. Personally, I am always ready for a full English breakfast after a night of strenuous and, though I say it myself, expert love making. Mmm, maybe I shouldn't be saying these things. Men! What are we like?

You probably realise by now that this is all tongue in cheek stuff, and I've only made these stupid sexist remarks to illustrate my point. Such point being, that there is no way us men are all the same. To bluntly say we are, in the categoric way that women tend to do, is far too much of a sweeping generalisation.

Take me for example. I am totally unlike other men. For a start, not many men have my good looks or my intelligence. Women find me irresistible. I can just tell by the way they look at me. The only reason I haven't had a girlfriend for many years, is because I hate to disappoint so many of you. Like most men, I am very thoughtful like that. My ex-wife was very wrong to say all those nasty things at the divorce hearing. Obviously, her emotional state must have got the better of her. Probably a touch of PMT. As for what my former mother-in-law said. Well, a lesser man would have sued. Not me though, I understand women. I'm just not the same as other men.

Here's yet another example of why I'm not like other men. I don't wear shorts when the sun shines.

It is early morning. The sun is about to take a look over the horizon, and the 'Wing Commander' my handsome cockerel, in glad expectation of another fine day, has begun to crow.

The reason I am sitting here at my keyboard so early, is that last night as I composed my blog, the computer crashed. I think it's called a crash. What happened was that the screen froze, and I was unable to continue writing. Which is a shame, because it was going to be a masterly diatribe about how women think all men are the same.

It happened once before this frozen screen business. Fortunately, my long-suffering friend and neighbour Steve was able to help me recover what I had written that time. But when it happened last night it was near midnight, and I thought he might not be best pleased at being dragged out of bed to help me at that hour.

However, all is not quite lost. Using the knowledge gained from Steve last time, I could save my masterpiece to a file, and there it sits. I can't recall how he showed me to bring it back. So, I must wait until he returns from work this evening. When hopefully, he will once again come to my rescue.

Now I can hear a rook's harsh call, and yes, there they go, the cooing of the collared doves. Not to be outdone a wood pigeons deeper note is quickly added. 'Lucky' the tame rescued crow is awake now, and caws a greeting.

The 'Wing Commander' has reached full throttle. I must go and open the hen house door so that he can perform his early morning nuptials. He is always up for it in the mornings. Takes me back to when I was a young man. No! I never used to chase hens around the paddock. You know what I mean.

Here is the sun now. Casting a red light through the window. Oh dear! Red sky in the morning. Shepherds warning. There is a bit of a breeze today after many days of warm stillness. I am being gently showered with petals from the cherry tree as it blows through the mollicroft windows. Mollicroft. Do you know that word? I'm going to leave you wondering.

Chaffinches have a monotonous one note call. But now it combines with the robin's happy sound and becomes part of the ever-rising dawn chorus. The wren is so loud for such a small bird, and here comes a blackbird, or is it a song thrush? It is both. I love this early morning orchestration.

There is a railway track at the bottom of the field, and a train has just fled past. I do not envy those early morning commuters. An empty tipper truck has just rumbled noisily over the level crossing.

Bonnie the cat is seeking my attention. I shall stroke her lovely head. Scratch her ears. She likes that. What she is really after though, is her breakfast. So am I.

I will have a couple of slices of buttered toast and marmalade. No, I won't! I will have an egg on toast, and another cup of tea. Then Sadie, the German Shepherd and I, shall have a nice walk across the back field, where she will unsuccessfully chase rabbits.

Then I shall take up my easel and go into town. Where I will hopefully make lots of money drawing portraits. Ha!

The world is waking up.

A mollicroft is a raised roof on a wagon or caravan, which gives extra headroom.

Hi, I'm Sadie the German Shepherd. I thought

I would have a go at this writing lark while John is in the toilet. He'll be there for ages reading the paper.

How long is he going to be? It's an age since he first announced that we were going out for a walk. He knows how excited I get when he comes out and says, "Where's your lead? Find it. Find your lead". We both know where the lead is. It's hanging in the tractor shed behind the door. But anyway, I humour him. So, off I go, running around like a maniac, and making stupid whiney noises of excitement. While he stands grinning inanely at my antics. Then he gets a bit worried that I'm going to jump up at him and scratch his face with my paws. "Calm down". He says. "Calm down". But we're going for a walk and it's not easy to calm down. He'll raise his voice then and shout, "NO SADIE. NO!" That calms me down.

He went through the gate, into Tricia's garden. He's keeping an eye on the puppies for her. I know there are puppies because I can smell them on him. I wish he would hurry up.

At last! He's coming back. He'll now do that daft thing of trying to get back through the gate without me hearing him. John! I'm a German Shepherd. I've got ears like a.. like a.. like a German Shepherd. I hear you. I could hear you even when you were in the house.

Is he going to the tractor shed? Yes! This could be it! Don't say it John. Please don't. But he does say it.

"Where's your lead? Find it. Find your lead".

Which means that I must go through the whole excited, going for a walk, routine again. I wish I could stop myself, but I can't. I'm a creature of habit and so is he. Except he would never admit it.

We go through the back gate into the big field. It has just been ridged and planted with potatoes, so the going is a bit tricky for a few hundred yards until we get to the proper footpath. It's on occasions like this, that I am reminded that John used to be a merchant seaman. The language! You wouldn't believe it.

The farmer has reinstated the footpath by flattening the ridges and we cut across this bit of the field without too much trouble for his old legs. It's a quick bit of walk and quite boring. Even so I manage to almost trip him a couple of times when I stop suddenly in front of him to investigate a smelly bit. He reminds me what my name is, "SADIE!"

Now we reach the road. I always stop here, because I know he will want to put my lead on. He tells me what a good girl I am. I love it when he says that, and we cross safely.

This is my favourite bit of the walk. He lets me off the lead and I love to run ahead. There are lots of rabbit holes to investigate and the smells! Well the smells are to die for, they really are. One day there was a decomposing hedgehog. Exquisite! I just had to roll in it. John was not pleased with me that day I can tell you. I had to suffer the dreaded hosepipe wash down. It was worth it though. I'd do it again.

Too soon we are next to the Church, and it is onto the lead again for the short stretch of road to the park. Oh no! Here comes a young mum pushing a pram. We will have to stop and say hallo. He says hallo to everyone we meet. A habit he picked up when he lived in a remote part of Scotland. It was all right up there, people were few and far between. But here in the south there are lots of people. On a busy day, he can take hours to get anywhere. He does smile and say hallo this time. Luckily for me she is not too responsive and we make it to the park, without me having to sit impatiently while he rattles on about something or other. These days it's usually the royal wedding. He can't wait to see 'the dress'. I made that bit up. Nothing flakey about our John.

In the park John watches me like a hawk. He gets worried you see. He thinks I am going to poop on the grass. Actually, I have already 'left a message' in the other field, but he doesn't trust me not to do it again. Sometimes, just for a bit of fun I pretend I'm getting ready to 'go'. "Don't you daaaarrre", he'll say in a stern voice, keeping it low in case anyone thinks he's a wicked dog owner. Honestly, he is hilarious.

This is nice. I think while he's watching I'll just bury my nose into this. He's getting worried. I recognise the signs.

Tense shoulders, slight frown. I'll just squat down. Give him a bit of a scare. He is rummaging in his pockets for a poop bag. Hilarious!

I am tied to a railing outside the shop, while he is buying a newspaper. The window cleaner wants to get this window next to me cleaned but he is frightened of me. I can always tell. You are going to have to wait Matey. If I know John, he is going to be chatting away in the shop for flipping ages. That's it, just work around me. Keep just outside my reach. I'm really vicious I am. I'm a German Shepherd.

That's strange. A bloke in a kilt! Don't see many of those in Sussex. Hope he doesn't stand around for too long. If John sees him, he will be bound to want to talk. He likes people who are a bit different.

Too late! He's been noticed. Off they go. Natter, natter, natter. Blimey, and he says women talk too much! I may as well have a lay down.

The Scotsman has gone at last. John probably wore him out. They were talking for ages trying to outdo each other on who's legs are the weakest. It's a bit like young men comparing tattoos, only it's for older people.

What a day this has been. Full of sentiment and

emotion for this particular old reprobate. There has been a royal wedding you see. What! You didn't know! I can't believe that! I'm sure it was advertised.

It's quite strange really, but I only seem to remember just how jingoistic I am when an event like this happens. Watching all that pomp and ceremony causes my aged, and probably cholesterol filled heart, to swell almost to bursting point, with pride. Are we the best at pomp and circumstance? I think we are. Who else is better?

Our American friends may know how to do a parade, letting their hair down, uninhibited, and really going for it. But we British, with our stiff upper lipped reserve. Well, we know how to do a cavalcade, a procession, an equitation, and a fanfare of trumpets without parallel. I may be a tiny bit biased of course. But what wonderful stuff. Full of history and tradition. Doesn't it give you hope for the future of our Great Britain?

Losing our heritage? Our culture? No way. Not if today is anything to go by. As for that minority of British folk who like to rubbish the whole event. Those who have the brass necked effrontery to malign our Royal family. Well. I do believe treason is still a capital offence. Hang 'em from the tower I say!

When the weather is fine. As it has been for some weeks, my television refuses to work. I think it is caused by atmospherics, and all the trees I have planted over the years. This is not normally much of a concern for me. But today, The Royal Wedding day. Well a bit of a disaster. So, I went to watch it with Tricia and my son George, at their house.

Tricia is my ex-partner and George's Mum. Her and I are still the best of friends, and the three of us are still able to do family things together, which works out very well. All in all, a very fine arrangement. I thought I would just share that with you. In line with my policy of keeping you informed as we move through my everyday musings.

Well, all the trees around here might spoil my television viewing, but I am nevertheless, extremely fond of them. I would like to question however, whether trees are actually needed inside Westminster Abbey. Isn't the building itself enough of an attractive thing to look at? This is just an observation on my part, not a criticism. But I was not consulted on the matter, so how were they to know?

I fear the arboreal overload was the doing of our 'Charlie'. Perhaps with his penchant for talking to plants he thought he might need something to share his thoughts with, during the quieter moments of the wedding. Or maybe the Queen requested them to keep the Corgi's happy. Before she realised that dogs wouldn't be allowed in anyway.

Her Majesty looked lovely, don't you think? Like a sweet little yellow canary. She always looks so well turned out. You have to wonder how she does it on her pension.

Prince Philip, still a handsome man at ninety years old. Seems that he has still got a twinkle in his eye for the ladies. The old devil.

Catherine's sister, I've forgotten her name for the moment, and I can't be bothered to look it up. What an absolute cracker she is. Prince Harry thought so too. I know it's part of the best man's duties to look after the chief bridesmaid, but blimey, he was attentive, didn't you think?

William looked quite nice in his fancy Irish Guards uniform. How did he get to be a Colonel at his age? I bet there was a bit of favouritism there. Know what I mean? Nudge, nudge. Probably knows someone high up at the Ministry of Defence. I'm saying nothing.

The bride, Catherine, a stunningly beautiful young woman. What can I say? You are a lucky young man William. But of course, you already know it. What with being a member of the Royal family, and all that.

Now here comes a criticism. Only a minor one though. It's just that I thought the Archbishop should have had a haircut and a beard trim. OK, I can forgive him the haircut bit. Though he did look as though he had been a bit over enthusiastic with the 'head and shoulders' shampoo. His hair looked as though it might fly away at any moment. Perhaps he forgot that he might have to take his hat off occasionally. Really Rowan, I know you favour the bohemian look, but this was a Royal wedding. Everyone else made a bit of an effort. A beard trim wouldn't have gone amiss. The eyebrows too. Crikey! How long have you been cultivating those beauties? Be honest now Rowan. How would you have felt, if the Queen had turned up looking like she had been dragged through a hedge backwards? Eh? Think about it Rowan. A bit more respect next time. The Queen is your boss, don't forget. I'll leave that little rant there. Don't want to spoil a nice day.

The wedding vows themselves seemed to pass off all right. Though I did feel that William rather rushed and mumbled his way through the bit, where he promises to share all his worldly goods. Probably he was trying to remember what he had said in the pre-nuptial agreement.

That's about it then. Royal wedding accomplished. No apparent mishaps. I wish the happy couple a long and happy marriage. Let's hope it lasts. I won't be putting any of my money on it though.

One morning shortly before my Mother

passed away, we were sitting at the table she and I. Mum had just had her breakfast, which at that time, was her usual repast of brandy and orange juice, cigarettes, and assorted prescription drugs. The brandy was what she always described as her morning tonic and the orange juice she mixed with it, she felt was necessary for the health-giving qualities contained in its vitamin C. The pills which she seemed to down in huge quantities, and with great regularity, were for her many ailments, whether real or imagined. Mum lived to be 84 years of age. So perhaps her breakfasts were not too bad.

This particular day she had risen early and the brandy bottle had taken even more of her interest than usual. I seem to recall her looking at the bottle a bit ruefully and blaming 'Fergie, the drunken bastard' for the bottles almost empty state. Fergie was my mother's long-time friend, my 'Uncle'.

She had something on her mind this morning. I knew this because she had called me her 'lovely boy'. Her 'good son' when I had joined her.

The alcohol had made her maudlin and she attempted, through her tears, and somewhat befuddled brain, to explain the reason for having me incarcerated -not too strong a word, I feel- in a residential children's home when I was a young boy.

The reason, to my Mothers way of thinking, was apparently very simple and easily explained. It seems that my Auntie Joe, her sister, wasn't able to have me. So, she thought it better to have me taken into care.

That was it. Nothing about the circumstances of the event. Why she couldn't keep me herself for example. Where she went. What she did. Who? What? Where? Why? Nothing.

This stumbling, tearfully inebriated explanation. This apology. Though brief, extremely brief, conveyed, unwittingly on her part, far more information to me, about the type of person she was, than she, in her drunken torpor, probably realised.

Mum was never, in the normal course of events, able to talk about the past. So, I judged this moment to be quite a significant one, in both our lives.

Although what she said, had hardly even scratched the surface of many issues I would have loved to know about. I felt that she was, in her own idiosyncratic way, pointing out to me, that the whole sorry state of affairs wasn't her fault.

Having reached well into my forties when this incident occurred, I had matured enough -although some people would dispute this- to be well aware of the setbacks that life can throw at you. Indeed, I had by this time family problems of my own. I knew a bit about fault and blame.

She loved me, my Mum. She just had a few problems. Some people can cope with things better than others, that's all.

One important thing she did. She made me a survivor.

Mum, I know it wasn't your fault. It wasn't anybody's fault. It's just life. It's that thing that happens in the long interval between being born and being dead.

I never judged you when I was a child. I don't judge you now. I loved you then and I love you still. These tears that fill my eyes today, are the tears I should have cried a long time ago. They are tears of relief, and slightly painful joy. How I wish we could have cried them together.

Maybe someday we will.

Now then, I am well aware that it is wrong to

laugh at other people's misfortunes. I am. I really am. It is absolutely wrong. Very naughty indeed. Not something I would ever do. Never! Who? Me? No!

But you must admit if you're honest, that it is quite funny if you happen to see for instance: a fat bloke stuck in a turnstile at the football ground. Even funnier if it's one of the away team supporters. What about when the bottom falls out of someone's carrier bag full of shopping? That's quite funny, isn't it? Someone having a hard time walking on an icy pavement. that is always good for a chuckle. Especially when they do that scampering along trying to keep their balance bit, before the inevitable happens and they land on their bottom. Quite funny that. Hilarious.

Don't you just love those TV shows where they delight in showing peoples misfortunes? You don't? Are you sure? I could have sworn I saw you suppressing a smile. Oh well, if you say you don't who am I to doubt you?

But anyway, as I was saying. I would never laugh at some unfortunate person's discomfort. Never!

Except today. When something happened that keeps making me chuckle to myself, every time I think about it.

Oh dear! Stop it! Just get on and tell the story! Sorry about that. Just giving myself a bit of a telling off.

Today, down at the local shop, I met a man who could only walk backwards. I didn't know he could only walk backwards when I started chatting to him, because he was standing still at the time. The subject came up in our conversation.

Apparently, what happened to this chap, was that one day as he was crossing the road, both his knees locked and he couldn't move. This of course was unfortunate. What made it even more disastrous for the poor bloke was that he was only halfway across when it happened. This is not funny. The road was very busy. So, he was stuck there for quite a long time. He was very worried. Well you would be, wouldn't you? About the traffic naturally, but mainly about his knees. They just would not bend.

He told me that he tried doing pelvic thrusts in an effort to gain some forward momentum, but had to give that up when he noticed a woman looking at him suspiciously and reaching for her mobile phone. Also, some drivers were winding down their windows and saying things, like pervert, and weirdo. Which is not very nice, but perhaps understandable. Especially when directed at a bloke, standing in the middle of a busy road, doing highly suggestive movements.

Eventually, after wracking his brains for some time. He hit upon the solution to his dilemma and walked backwards to where he had started. Which as he said himself, was a very dodgy thing to do, because passing motorists couldn't tell if he was coming or going.

He walked backwards all the way home, and because he had to keep stopping and shuffling around to see where he was going, people were making nasty comments as he made his awkward progress.

To cap it all off he told me that when he finally got home his wife gave him short shrift because he hadn't got the shopping. When he explained about his knees she called him a daft old fool.

The operation to try and sort out his knees had not been successful. He was going to go back into hospital soon, for another go, but in the meantime, was still having to walk backwards.

The police stop him a lot apparently. Wanting to know what he's up to. He's getting fed up with them. But as he says, it's a free country. There's no law against walking backwards.

Because he was facing the door I assumed that he was just leaving.

"Are you going"? I asked him. Thinking I might offer him a lift home.

"No", he said. "I've just arrived", and with that he walked off. Backwards.

It is the summer of nineteen hundred and

sixty-three. The Beatles and the Rolling Stones are just starting out on their incredible journeys to fame and fortune. I too am on a journey. Without the fame or the fortune sadly. I have almost completed a long, long train ride from Aberdeenshire, in bonny Scotland. Here I am at last. Sharpness railway station in Gloucestershire within reach of my destination, the Merchant Navy training establishment, TS Vindicatrix.

There were quite a few of us youngsters milling about the station entrance, with our various bags and suitcases. Some of the boys had obviously met up on the train and were in groups of two or three, being quite loud. Their new-found friendships lending them a bravado which others, including myself were not feeling.

Standing alone, slightly bewildered as to what to do next, most of us were nervously and inexpertly puffing on cigarettes.

We exchanged glances. Sizing each other up. Who looked friendly? Who best to avoid? Tentative smiles. A greeting. "Alright?"

"Yeah. You alright?"

"Yeah mate. I'm alright"

I'm sure that most of us weren't feeling alright, but we soon relaxed into each other's company. Kindred spirits embarking on a journey into the unknown.

A bus with a roughly scribbled notice on the windshield, TS VINDICATRIX, pulls into the station forecourt and out jumps a tough looking man wearing a naval uniform. He greets us warmly. "You can put those fucking fags out for a fucking start."

Impressed with his commanding use of the English language we hasten to obey.

He impresses us even further. "Now pick those fucking cases up and go and stand in two lines over there." Indicating with his pointing finger where over there is. "And get a fucking move on."

In our nervous rush to please, we make a right mess of lining up in two's, provoking more seaman like vernacular. But eventually, by the brute force of his winning personality, our new-found friend and mentor, manages to get us lined up, counted, and on the bus.

Five minutes later we arrive at the Merchant Navy Training Establishment, TS Vindicatrix, Sharpness, Gloucestershire, England.

At sixteen years of age my dream of becoming a merchant seaman is about to be realised. A dream which is soon to be a nightmare of dreadful food, early morning wake ups, exhausting physical exercise, marching routines and any other hellish thing you can think of that might cause a rebellious teenage youth to have second thoughts about his chosen career path.

Our quarters were long wooden huts. The kind of things you would see in prisoner of war films. In fact, for the next three months this was a prison, for if we wanted to complete the course we would not be allowed outside this camp, except for two days 'leave' in the last week.

It was to be a very tough regime. A lot of lads were not prepared to put up with it and soon gave up. Quite a few of them would not last even one day. How they thought they would manage for months at sea I have no idea.

One boy. A bit of a 'Jack the Lad' was shown the door, when on being asked to declare his religion, he answered that he was an atheist. We were expected to be God fearing. No place for a non-believer at sea apparently. Can you imagine that happening today? Unthinkable. Superstitious lot sailors. Doesn't really make much sense if you ask me. After all, if the good Lord is looking after you, what is the point of being superstitious. Still better safe than sorry.

I didn't have any worries about completing the course. This place was just another institution and I was very well used to that. No, I had a much bigger concern than that. I had a concern that had traumatised me for days. I was very worried about my underpants!

My clothing at this time was still being bought for me by the children's department. In the shape of my welfare officer. They call them social workers these days. She was a stickler for the rules this one and insisted that I have the regulation, old fashioned flannel underwear. I wanted Y fronts. I begged her for Y fronts. But no, she would not budge!

That woman! The angst she caused me. Those flannel underpants were longer than the regulation PE shorts and hung down below them for everyone to see. Oh, the cringing embarrassment!

I've forgotten a lot about my time at the TS Vindicatrix, but I will never forget those underpants. Honestly, I'm still traumatised today. Maybe I should have some counselling.

I wish to apologise for the Chief Petty Officers bad language.

Richard was, until his retirement a few

months ago, a warder at the prison just across the fields from here. Probably less than a mile as the crow flies.

One day not too long ago, Sadie the German Shepherd and I bumped into him on our walk.

"Hi Rich", I greeted him. "How's things?"

Richards normal morose expression changed to exceedingly morose. "I'm bloody well annoyed."

As Sadie, and Richards black Labrador Jack, conducted a detailed analysis of each other's rear quarters. He told me that he was so fed up, he was seriously contemplating selling up and moving away from the area. The thing which had brought about this thinking on his part, was that every day when he looked out of his kitchen window, he was confronted with the sight of one of his former clients, sitting on the grass verge opposite his house. In this hyper sensitive politically correct age I knew that when he used the word 'client' he was in fact referring to an ex prisoner.

Due to client confidentiality Richard was not able to go into any more detail. I commiserated with him. Said goodbye, and Sadie and I went on our way.

Two or three days after this exchange, Tricia, my friend and former partner, told me that she was thinking of employing someone to come and help her in the garden for a few hours a week. On hearing this I went through my usual spiel of telling her it wasn't necessary to employ someone, as I was always available to help. Having heard this before, she laughed, thanked me for my kind offer, and told me she was going ahead with her plan anyway.

I didn't like the new gardener at all. He seemed a bit smarmy, and a bit too familiar if you ask me. He was there more than a few hours a week too. Once I overheard him tell Tricia to make a cup of tea for them both and come and have a sit down. The cheeky bastard. Added to that, he never even had any garden tools of his own. Always wanting to borrow mine. Normally I have this maxim. If you need to borrow something more than three times, then you probably need to buy one for yourself. In this case though, because it was helping Tricia I let him get away with it.

Move forward a few days. I get a phone call from Tricia. She wants me to call round to the house. It is urgent. She sounds upset, so of course I hurry round to see what the problem is.

Richard has been around. He is concerned for her. The new gardener is one of his former clients. The one who has been sitting on the grass verge outside his house every day.

The new gardener is out on licence from prison. The new gardener is a double wife murderer!

Understandably Tricia has changed her mind. She doesn't want anyone helping in the garden. She is worried and frightened and doesn't know what to do, how to get rid of him.

Gallantly, and with extreme heroism, if I do say so myself. I offer to tell him to go away.

"No"! She says. "He might kill you"!

"He won't kill me". I tell her. Adding thoughtfully. "He only kills women."

"You mustn't say anything to upset him. He might come back and stab me in the night".

After I have reassured her with the thought that he only kills women he is married to. We hit upon the solution to this somewhat tricky situation. Tricia will simply tell him that her financial circumstances have changed, and she cannot afford to pay him.

It turns out that this man uses a technique known as passive aggression to get his way. He is extremely good at it. It is a technique which a well-mannered person, such as Tricia would find hard to resist. It relies on a person being simply unable to know how to tell the aggressor to go away. It is somewhat similar to the methods that might be used by a high-pressure salesman.

This man is now back inside and awaiting trial for the attempted murder of his new partner.

To conclude. If you are thinking about employing someone you don't know to prune your roses, I offer the following piece of sound advice. Think again!

Auntie May has shut me in the cupboard under

the stairs. Difficult for me to remember the reason why on this occasion, because there were so many misdemeanours it was possible to commit. Though most of the things we got up to which were considered bad enough to merit punishment, were in fact just us kids being kids.

My regular and most featured crime however, was not being able to eat macaroni cheese. I lived in fear and trepidation of macaroni cheese day. What day it was precisely I cannot recall. All I know is, that it came around relentlessly every week, and every week I knew I was going to be tormented by a plateful of this disgusting concoction.

Try as I might I could not get it down. Auntie May would get angrier and angrier as she watched me picking at it. She was so determined I would empty my plate, that she would resort to holding my nose as she attempted to shovel the muck down my reluctant throat. It was all to no avail. My gagging reflex would kick in and the battle would be over for the moment. Off I would go to the cupboard. Where I think, I was supposed to reflect on my crime.

What Auntie May didn't realise, was that after my initial fears had subsided, I was quite happy being imprisoned in this cupboard, among the mops and brushes and other sundry cleaning materials. As far as I was concerned this was quite a nice little haven. Away from the petty squabbles and upsets of life in a children's home. Even in the pitch darkness my eyes would somehow find enough light for me to fashion a pillow out of dusters and cleaning cloths and snuggle down, engulfed in the scent of carbolic soap, for a few hours' peaceful sleep.

She was however a determined woman, and often, the next day would find me confronted with the same plateful of food for breakfast, dinner and tea.

Being able to adapt to this punishment was to serve me well a few years down the line, when I was left in the care of a monstrous foster 'mother'. A foster 'mother' with a cellar. I'll keep her for another time.

Not everyone was as adaptable as me in these circumstances. Being left alone in the dark is a very common and terrifying childhood fear. It was extremely worrying for us youngsters to have to watch one of our peers being dragged kicking and screaming to the cupboard. It sets off a sense of helplessness in a child when it is realised how powerless they are to prevent suffering. This compounds a feeling of worthlessness in children. Some of whom are already deeply troubled by unpleasant circumstances in their young lives.

It is not an excuse, but to my mind, inflicting these unthinking and traumatising punishments on children in care is the reason so many of us would go off the rails. I include myself in this. Maybe it is an excuse.

As I sit here today, thinking back over a troubled childhood, I am filled with incredulity that grown people in a supposedly caring profession could act in this abhorrent way. Quite astonishing how many people who dislike kids choose childcare as a career. Or am I being incredibly naive? How I wish it was possible to confront them with their crimes.Tell them what I thought of them then. What I think of them now.

I am off out now. Been invited to dinner. Hope I mentioned that I don't like macaroni cheese!

"NEWS 'n' STANNAD. NEWS 'n' STANNAD".

Old Tom and I are standing beside a newspaper stand. He is trying to teach me how to shout out the name of the papers. We are selling the London Daily News and the Evening Standard. I don't want to shout. It's embarrassing. I've never been one to draw attention to myself.

"Right orft you go Johnny boy. Loud as yer can. Go on".

Self-consciously I give it a go. "News and Standard".

"Gor stone me. Did yer say somefink Johnny boy? Do it agin, a lot bleedin' louder. Come on, Lord bleedin' Nelson wants to ere' yer".

Lord Nelson was looking down at us from his column in Trafalgar Square across the road. Old Tom and I were situated beside Admiralty Arch in Whitehall. It was a prime spot for selling papers and Old Tom and my newly found older brother Vic were really pleased to have the permit for it.

I grew to really enjoy selling papers here. Even got brave enough to shout out the odd headline or two.

"READ ALL ABOUT IT! READ ALL ABOUT IT! JURY OUT IN CHATTERLEY TRIAL. READ ALL ABOUT IT!"

I loved watching all the posh gentlemen in their bowler hats, coming and going from the Admiralty. Lots of them became regular customers and they were very good tippers too. Most would give me an extra penny. Some of them would give me sixpence for a threepenny paper and say, "keep the change young fellow." Sometimes I'd even get to keep the change from a shilling. But that was quite rare.

We also had the concession to sell papers and sweets in the Charing Cross hospital just down the road. It was fun to push the trolley around the wards. People were really nice, and always seemed pleased to see me. So, as you can see life was not all misery.

This part of my life's tapestry took place when I was about eleven years old. It was a happy time, because I got to know my brother Vic who was a lot older than me. He was quite a character. Full of fun and confidence. Having him around was fantastic. It was wonderful to have someone on my side for a change.

Vic and Old Tom also had a bookshop in Camberwell and I would help out. It wasn't a very busy place, but I loved books and was happy to be there.

It was in this tiny little back street bookshop that I, at the tender age of eleven made history, when I became the youngest person in the whole world, or so Vic told me, to sell one of the first ever copies of the newly legal, Lady Chatterley's Lover. Which I believe was a kind of instruction manual for gamekeepers. Apparently, a lot of readers, mainly male, skipped this bit. It was certainly a book which opened my eyes very wide, and taught me a lot. Though of course it would be some years before I could put theory into practice.

These happy times came to a sudden end when Old Tom ran off with all the money. Vic had to find another way of making a living.

He chose to take the Queens shilling and joined the army. It was a sad time. I didn't see him again for many years.

Vic may have left a big void in my life, but he also enriched it hugely. This short period in my life is something I love to think back on. Me. Making history. Who'd have thought it? I have such a lot to thank my big brother for.

I would also like to take this opportunity to say a great big thank you, to Mr D.H. Lawrence, and Penguin books, for helping me to become such an accomplished and versatile lover.

After my extremely handsome Son,

George had left school, I soon came to realise the next phase of his life was not going to be so reliant on me. All right he still needs his Dad to drive him about, but the places he goes do not include me being involved. Nowadays he goes to football matches with his friends. I have no idea when I will get the chance to beat him at snooker again. In fact, he even goes to a different snooker club. As for our camping trips. I suspect they are a thing of the past too. On our regular walks to look at nature, his young eyes were a great help in spotting things my own old eyes would miss. Nowadays I must remember to take a pair of binoculars with me.

That's OK. I'm pleased he is becoming his own person. I'm glad that he has friends that he likes to spend time with. It did leave quite a gap in my life however. I needed to get on with things for myself. I needed to, 'get a life', as they say.

For some years, I have been trying to learn to play the guitar. I say trying because at my advanced stage of decay it is not easy. Actually, I discovered that the guitar is quite fiendishly difficult. Not least, it requires an ability to coordinate both hands to do separate things but at the same time. It is something obviously, which is best started young. When brain cells still have the ability to learn easily. It is also something which requires an awful lot of practice. I have not practiced enough. After eleven years, I am still rubbish at it.

But, let me tell you, all is not lost. I have discovered the fun to be had at an open mic night. The open mic nights are becoming more and more popular and are now a regular part of the more discerning, great British Public House. They give anyone who wants to, a chance to get up and entertain.

Well I suppose the reason I wanted to learn the guitar was to entertain. Although I have to say, for some strange reason I have never been able to figure out, nobody ever had the time to listen to me sing and play. Whenever I would suggest getting my guitar out, people would make excuses that they had to be somewhere else. Very odd. I have been told I have a beautiful voice. Well they may have said, interesting, rather that beautiful. But they mean the same thing, Don't they?

Thank goodness though for 'Open mic with Sedge and Jon'. Two Maestro guitarists. Two brilliantly gifted virtuoso performers. Two young -relatively speaking- men of spectacular ability. (Is this all right guys. Can I stop now?)

On Sedge and Jon's poster it invites anyone to join in. So, it is their own fault that I now regularly go along. They are so welcoming, and I have made many new friends. Even though I never buy a round of drinks.

Apparently, my open mic performances attract so many people that a contract is being written up stating that I must always appear. I never knew about this until last night when I was told about it, by a bloke who wanted me to lend him a tenner. This is very moving, and I am filling up with emotion, just thinking about how far I have come as an entertainer. Thank you so much you guys.

There is a downside though. Of course, there is. There would have to be wouldn't there? As soon as women hear me sing they become hysterical. Fainting and swooning have become commonplace among my female fans. To be honest I have even seen blokes standing there, staring open mouthed in disbelief at my musical ability. Lots of people get so excited that they have to leave early. I may have to tone my act down a bit. I'm beginning to feel a bit like Elvis. You know what happened to him.

So, that's it. This is my social life now that George is not so reliant on me. It seems that I have become a phenomenon. People whisper my name whenever I appear. They don't need to whisper, I know what they are saying. All I can say is thank you. I appreciate it very much. I do not intend to let this newfound fame change me in any way. It is so hard to be humble when you are perfect. But somehow, I will manage it.

You can see Open Mic with Sedge and Jon at www.myspace.com/play_live. They are on Facebook too. You might even see and hear me singing. But please have your smelling salts ready.

Just a few days ago, I was bemoaning

the fact that my extremely handsome young son George, wasn't interested in going to the snooker club with me anymore. So, it came as a bit of a surprise when he suddenly announced a desire to accompany me to that very place.

Oh, let joy be unconfined! George's simple request made my heart leap and soar with happiness. How I would delight in beating him on the green baize once again. When I say beating him, I don't mean that I hold him down physically and beat him with a stick or a paddle. I would never do that. Not even when, during one of our friendly wrestling bouts, he chances his luck, and has that look. The look that tells me he thinks he can take on his old Dad and win. He is taller and probably stronger than me now, but no son. Not just yet.

Driving to the snooker club we are delayed behind a woman cyclist. Not normally a subject worth commenting on. However, I could not fail to notice, even with my failing eyesight, that she was wearing, what I think are called leggings, but look like tights. Those stretchy things, which look very nice on the slimmer feminine figure, but which take on a somewhat less pleasing aspect when worn by women of a more, shall I say, Rubenesque form.

Let me hasten to add at this point, that I am very fond of the amply proportioned woman. I enjoy a cuddle as much as the next man. But I do feel that the larger lady wearing stretchy green tights, should perhaps not be wobbling along a busy road on a racing bike. Especially when those tights are stretched to their maximum loading capacity and have, in the process become see through. Thereby revealing her underwear. It must be thoroughly uncomfortable wearing a thong when cycling. A white thong, with a label on it, stating that it was bought in a well-known department store.Although the lady should be admired for what looked like a determined effort to get fit, I feel it is a dangerous way to do it.

Now the reason I am relating this incident is of course purely in the interest of road safety. A lesser man than I could very easily be distracted enough by a sight like this, to cause a road traffic accident. Not me though! Although I was stuck behind this lady for some time, I am proud to say that I managed to avert my eyes quite a lot. But not before being reminded of an oil painting by Turner. I can't recall the paintings title, but it is the one which depicts a pale moon rising from a turbulent green sea!

When George and I arrive at the snooker hall, he reminds me that it is time to pay our annual membership dues. A fact which makes me a wee bit suspicious of my dear boy's motive in inviting me to play. But no, he is not a devious young man. Not at all. I pay up happily. Pleased to be in his company once more. We play two games. Of course, I let him win the first game, and only narrowly let him win the second. After all I don't want to knock his confidence.

Suddenly four of George's friends arrive. Unfortunately, they don't have enough money to pay for a table but they wouldn't mind a game or two.

I leave my son happily playing snooker with his pals, and drive home alone. Wondering how an inexpensive outing with him has left me without enough cash in my pocket for fish and chips. Wondering also why his friends turned up if they had no money.

It was a lovely couple of hours though. Well worth it. Emotionally I mean, not financially.

An apology: My account of the woman on the bike has me cringing. I am ashamed that I thought it OK to poke fun at her. I could have deleted it, but I am leaving it in as a reminder to myself to always consider other's feelings.

My legs are weak. My knees are

buckling. Oh help! What is going on here? My head is swimming. Looking up at the high ceiling it appears that the lights are spinning crazily. I am going to fall.

Concerned faces loom over me as I regain consciousness. Someone picks me up and carries me to an empty classroom. A sit down and a drink of water later I am feeling better.

The school nurse asks me what had been wrong. My six-year-old mind struggles for an answer. All I can come up with by way of explanation is that I had an empty hollow feeling inside.

It seems that morning assembly at school had overwhelmed me, and I had fainted. That's all it was. The heat probably, and the lights, had got to me. If only I had been able to state it so simply all those years ago. But I couldn't. As I say I was only six years old.

Several days later, the housemother -this is a children's home- tells me that I am to hurry and put my best clothes on. I have been summoned to the main office. Usually this happens because some prospective foster parents have arrived to give me the once over. See if I meet their requirements. My own requirements, even if I could think of any, don't come into it. Several people have looked me over, but I haven't been chosen yet. Does a lot for a child's self-esteem, this process. Anyway, I don't want to go anywhere. I've got a Mum. Somewhere.

My best clothes are the same as my normal clothes, gray. Except that they are newer and have not been subjected to repeated washing and mending. I have to wear shoes instead of the usual hob nailed boots. Oh yes, and I must wear a tie. I hate ties. In fact, anything which involves tying a knot or bow causes me concern. I can never tie anything up properly. Apparently, being able to do things like tie shoelaces or neckties should be simple for a small boy. I invariably get a cuff around the ear due to my lack of these essential life skills.

The cuff around the ear punishment is meted out on a regular basis for small, so called misdemeanours. Things like having elbows on the table at mealtimes. Or holding your knife and fork wrongly. Using the fork upside down to eat peas is very wrong. Deciding suddenly, that you need to go to the toilet. Not sitting up straight. Not realising that you are being spoken to. There are so many ways to irritate an impatient adult. The cuff around the ear is apparently an essential commonplace practice.

When administered with full on venom and uncontrolled anger, it then becomes a heavy smack around the head and is highly dangerous. Probably the cause of a great deal of brain damage. Hey! That explains a lot.

There are no prospective foster parents on this day. Instead I am ushered into the office of Mr Stevenson, the deputy superintendent of the home. He glares at me over the top of his wire framed glasses, "Stand up straight boy".

I have only ever seen this man from afar. He has a fearsome reputation. I am about to experience it for myself. "So, this is the boy we don't feed properly, is it?" He is looking at me, but his words are obviously addressed to the housemother. I sense that I am in trouble for something. I am right.

It seems that the school nurse has reported my fainting episode. My childish explanation has been misconstrued. She has reported me as being undernourished and hungry. This has caused a heap of trouble for the housemother. Mr Stevenson obviously does not like his staff to be criticised. He takes it personally. A loud and frightening verbal onslaught begins

Perhaps I tried to explain. But I was in fear of this man. He shouted a lot. Accused me of being ungrateful for all that was done for me. Anything I may have said would not have helped. We kids were, as the old saying goes, expected to be seen and not heard. I was left in no doubt that the whole situation was all my own fault.

The punishment for my 'crime' was that I must have double rations at every meal. For a picky eater like me this was very difficult. Luckily the ordeal only lasted a week. But it was a week of much crying and upset on my part, and much anger and intolerance from the housemother. Her right hand was well used that week.

It was only a faint for God's sake! I still don't know what caused it. But I'm sure I wasn't hungry. Well, not for the food they dished up to us ungrateful little wretches anyway.

Here is a short story inspired by

seeing a teddy bear tied to a dustcart's radiator grill.

Dirty, wet, limp, dull eyed and hung by the neck from the radiator grill of the local dustcart with a length of baler twine, the big yellow teddy bear did not have much going for it.

For a short time when the bear had first been found it was proudly displayed as a trophy on the cart. There had been no malice in this act. Albert Smith the refuse man who had rescued it from a dustbin, had simply wanted to personalise his truck.

Unfortunately, as the days had gone by, he and his workmates had quickly forgotten all about the bear. Despite its prominent position on the front of the vehicle, familiarity had soon bred in the men a form of mental blindness. They saw and yet they did not see. A common enough human failing.

Rain, hail, sleet and snow had all wreaked their havoc on the yellow teddy bear in the weeks since it had been tied to the cart, not to mention the battering it took on the journey to and from the refuse tip twice a day.

Albert Smith a widower, had, unbeknown to him, an admirer. A spinster, in her middle years, who had taken a keen interest in him from the first day she had seen him going about his work in his usual no nonsense way.

The lady in question, a Miss Violet Parsons was particularly taken with what she had observed to be Albert's kindly nature and his gentle ways. Not to mention his good looks and distinguished greying hair. She liked the way he always had time for a spoken pleasantry or a smile for young and old alike. Her admiration had increased even further the day she spotted Albert rescue the yellow teddy bear from a neighbours bin and carefully tie it to the grill of his truck.

Miss Parsons a schoolteacher, would often run the risk of being late for work on a Monday morning, just so she could catch a glimpse of Albert doing his rounds. The lovely lady was quite besotted, and yet so shy and tongue-tied in his presence that she found herself quite unable to respond to his always cheery, "good morning."

Albert who had not the slightest idea that he was so ardently admired, took her silence as a sign that she perhaps felt unable to bring herself to converse with a lowly dustman. However, he believed in treating everyone with the same respect whatever their background or position in life, and so he continued to be his usual self.

One Monday morning, Violet was standing beside her living room window, in happy anticipation of the dustcarts imminent appearance at the corner of her street. The day has begun kindly, and she noticed that the first crocus had opened in her small front garden. She was pleased. She saw the bright yellow flower as the first tangible sign that Winter was ending, and that Spring was in the air.

The colour yellow had also been a factor in Albert's start to the day. Not a yellow flower but a yellow teddy bear. The same hapless bear which had been tied to the grill of his truck for several weeks had chosen this particular day to make its sad sorry state known to him. Shocked to discover the plight of the bear Albert took matters in hand.

So it was that this morning, the teddy, who had been named Trashcan, found itself sitting, in a position of honour, on the dashboard of Albert's Dustcart.

Unfortunately, Trashcan's troubles were not yet over. The powerful heater above which it was seated had begun to dry the bear out. The stitching was rapidly coming apart. Trashcan was in great danger of falling apart.

As fate would have it, Trashcans dilemma was spotted by Albert just as he was pulling up outside Violet's house. Without seeming to think about the matter Albert carefully wrapped his big hands around the bear and jumped from the cab.

Violet from her position by the window was surprised to see Albert ignore her dustbin and continue to her front door, which he began to knock.

As she opened the door Albert held the yellow bear out to her. "I wonder have you got a carrier bag I can put him in?" He asked, bending to retrieve an arm that had fallen to the ground. "He's falling to pieces."

Carefully Violet reached out and took the bear from him. She was touched by his concern and the fact that he had given the bear a gender. "I'd like to see if I can repair him," she said shyly, "look, I think your friends are waiting."

Albert turned to see his workmates staring at him open mouthed. He had a feeling that this was going to be a hard one to live down.

"Thanks for your help then Mrs...?"

Please call me Violet," she said, adding, "and its Miss. Can you call by in a few days for the teddy bear?"

Thus, began a true romance, leading to marriage and a happy life for all concerned. Even a yellow teddy bear by the name of Trashcan.

It is twenty minutes past five in the

morning. I only went to bed at one o'clock and I have lain awake for an hour reflecting on my life thus far. So only three hours sleep and yet I am wide awake. All this without the help of the 'Wing Commander' my handsome golden cockerel, who has only now begun to crow his welcome to the new day. A day which is emerging lethargically, rather than the bright pleasantness we have grown used to in the first few weeks of this early Spring. It is grey outside. A grey to suit my mood this morning.

Very occasionally I am crushed by an overbearing weight of sadness at the way my life has transpired. This morning I feel it strongly. I have been thinking of family mostly. My mother. A Dad I never got to meet. Three brothers and a sister. None of whom I really got to know terribly well. They are gone now. My brother Victor and my sister Marian, both a lot older than me, I knew a little. I loved them both and had the privilege to tell them this. Even so, we could hardly be described as close. Alistair, just a year older than me, was a half-brother I never got to meet. He died young, still a boy. Brian is, or was, another half-brother. He disappeared as soon as he was old enough to survive on his own. I often wonder about him.

Many years ago, I had some kind of a nervous breakdown. The Doctors gave me pills, and I would every week or so, go and talk to a psychologist. My wife told me later that I spent most of the next three months in bed, refusing to see any visitors.

I ended this period of depression suddenly one day, when in a period of lucidity, I came to my senses, and decided to take back control of my life. The pills were flushed down the toilet. I never took one again. Whether the medication or the psycho analysis helped I cannot say with any certainty. Perhaps it did. But I like to think my well-honed survival instinct kicked in, and I healed myself.

Nonetheless for that, I got better quickly and life became 'normal' again.

What this breakdown did I think was to take a great load off me. Introspection took a back seat. Lots of bad memories loosened their grip, and sank into the background of my mind. I stopped feeling so sorry for myself. Stopped being so needy. Most importantly I was able to brush the chips off my shoulders. Take stock of how lucky I was compared to the sad plight of so many others around the world.

These days I do not allow unhappiness to reign free over my emotions, but as I say, it does occasionally rear its ugly head. This morning it has crept up on me. Held me for an hour or so, but now I will shake it away.

Sadie, the German Shepherd and I, shall go for an early morning walk.

"Come on Sadie, where's your lead? Find it girl! Find it!"

During the course of today, when I

should have been out drawing portraits, Sadie the German Shepherd and I went for a walk to the village. Nothing very exciting happened.

I did get a soaking as we passed by the huge sprinkler system which has been crawling up and down the rows of potatoes. In fact, as it has been such a hot day I found it quite refreshing. Well, all right to be honest with you, I walked under the spray deliberately. Sometimes I behave like a big kid. I tried to persuade Sadie to join me but she is far too intelligent. It wasn't until after I had refreshed myself in this way that I began to worry about what might have been added to the water. Suppose it had fertiliser in it. Or worse, some horrid chemicals. I had a good sniff of myself and, oh my word, I smelt terrible. However, on reflection, I decided that I didn't smell any worse than I normally do. So, I carried on with the walk.

Inspired by nature blogs, I had my camera with me, and so when I spotted a couple of ladybirds I attempted to photograph them. I say that I spotted the ladybirds. This is true in one way and false in another. They already had their spots when I spotted them. The spots were none of my doing. They were spotted ladybirds. It might have been possible, if I'd had a paint brush and some paint with me, that I would be able to add spots. But I didn't. The spots are genuine. I'm going to get off the subject of ladybirds for now. It's getting out of hand. Anyway, they are very small insects and I can't even see them in the photo.

On reaching the park and still being of a mind to capture some nature shots I became excited when I spotted, no not spotted, noticed, a bee entering a buttercup. Quickly ordering Sadie into the sit and stay position I dropped to my knees. I must remember not to do that again. My knees don't like it. Very painful. However, I was down now and slowly and carefully crept up on the bee. Oh dear! I do wish people would clean up after their dogs. The bee must have flown off as I was setting my camera to close up. Never mind, I'll try again tomorrow. I made a mental note of the time. Hopefully that bee is a creature of habit.

Despite my creaking knees, I managed to catch up with Sadie, who had completely disobeyed my order to sit and stay. She had been tempted by a strong desire to sniff at the rear end of a passing spaniel. I understand strong urges, so I let her off with just a mild scolding in this instance. The spaniel's elderly owner had sadly got herself worked up into a bit of a strop, and surprised me by employing the descriptive talents of a drunken sailor, as she explained exactly what she would like to do to my big brute of a dog. Really madam! A little decorum please.

So, it was that Sadie and I made it to the village shop. Where, using the knowledge gained from years of service as a merchant mariner I managed, after several attempts to secure her lead to the bike rack. Sadie always looks sad and forlorn when I leave her like this. So, I was not surprised to find as I left the shop, that she was being fussed over by an attractive woman. This happens a lot with Sadie, and it is always women who are attracted to her. I have not yet worked out a strategy for deflecting this attention away from Sadie and on to me, but it is something I am actively working on. Perhaps if I tied myself to the bike rack... Hmm! Might be worth a try.

Another chance for a fantastic nature shot occurred as we made our way back across the park. I saw a pair of birds sitting on the grass. They may have been standing. I couldn't be sure as they were some distance away. Camera at the ready I tried to look nonchalant and uninterested as I drew nearer. One of the birds saw straight through this bit of trickery, and flew off, but to my surprise the other one stayed where it was. I got within a few metres and it very kindly allowed me to take several photos before Sadie came galloping along and finally the bird saw sense and took off. It's so easy this nature photography. Obviously, the secret is to pretend you haven't noticed your quarry. Simple!

Sadie's claws had scratched me yesterday as she asked for a biscuit, so we walked the rest of the way home on the pavement. I think the tarmac makes a good job of filing her sharp claws down, and it saves me struggling with the nail clippers. She is not fond of having her nails clipped.

Unfortunately,this way home allowed Tricia to see me coming and gave her a chance to ask me to fix her bike which had got stuck in gear. I got Sadie safely home and turned my attention to the bike. After a couple of hours, it was fixed enough for her to ride, and she cycled off to work.

I was by now ready for a cup of tea, and had just put the kettle on when the phone rang. It was my handsome son George needing to be picked up from the station. Good heavens! Is it that time already? How time does fly.

George wanted a football kickabout when I got him home. I don't like to miss these rare opportunities to spend time with him, so we spent a happy hour or so as I demonstrated my phenomenal skill as a footballer.

He then went off to have something to eat, and I was finally able to make myself a nice cup of tea.

Suddenly it was time for me to get ready for open mic night at the pub. I hadn't eaten for hours and decided that I would eat something at the pub as I had no time to prepare anything. The kitchen at the pub was shut by the time I arrived. However, despite my hunger pangs the evening was very enjoyable.

Now I am back home. Not much to eat here either but I managed to rustle up a cheese and onion sandwich. A wonderful concoction to go to bed on. The indigestion has already kicked in.

That's about it then. Another productive day over. So, I will wish you goodnight. I must get to bed. There is a busy day ahead tomorrow. I shall get such a lot done.

Last Wednesday I decided that I needed to

see the Doctor. This was an unusual thing for me. I don't normally do ill health. But I have been having headaches and a feeling I can only describe as like a hangover. A 'spaced out' not quite with it, fuzziness. A sense of impending doom.

"We don't have any ordinary appointments available until two weeks' time", the Doctors receptionist informed me as she tapped my details into the computer.

"What's an ordinary appointment?" I enquired.

"None urgent." She answered. "Do you need an urgent appointment?"

"I'm not sure."

"Well how ill are you?"

"I don't know. I was hoping that the Doctor could tell me?"

More tapping on the keyboard. "Monday. Ten forty-five."

"Thank you. Is that ordinary or urgent?" I asked.

"It's a cancellation." She said. "You're a very lucky man."

Leaving the surgery, and thinking about how very lucky I am. I headed for the local shop and bought two lucky dip lottery tickets. I suppose I only needed one lucky ticket really. But I believed the receptionist when she informed me how lucky I am, and in my befuddled state I decided to double up. After all I'm so lucky that I would probably win twice.

The spaced out and fuzzy headed feeling continued for the rest of that day. On Thursday I could function a little better, but the headache came back when I returned from an evening out. On Friday, the fuzziness and spaced out, feeling of impending doom returned with a vengeance, and I took to my bed for most of the day.

This morning, Saturday. I woke feeling that I had done ten rounds in the ring with Mike Tyson. If this had happened of course I would have knocked him out in about round three. No contest. But anyway, my head was ringing fit to bust. I held my head under the cold tap trying to clear it. But to no avail. Next time I will try turning the tap on!

George, my extremely handsome son came visiting at about midday. "There is a horrible smell of gas in here Dad," he said, as he came through the door.

"Sorry about that son." I said. "It must be the Fava beans I had with liver, and a nice bottle of Chianti last night." I always have to make a joke. Even when I'm feeling like death.

George didn't laugh at my joke. "Can't you smell it Dad?"

Well I had noticed a strong smell. But to be honest, I thought it was coming from an onion that I had chopped and left in the fridge. I had found the lid was not on the container properly. I thought the smell was permeating from that.

Close investigation revealed that when I had fitted the new butane gas bottle some days previously I had failed to connect it properly and it had been leaking out.

I am so stupid! I thought when I fitted it that it hadn't gone on correctly, but because gas was coming through to the cooker I just assumed it must be all right.

The situation is now rectified. I am still a bit light headed, but improving all the time, thank the good Lord, as the toxicity leaves my body.

I am so pleased that when I built this wagon, I put the bedroom at the other end from the kitchen. I could have died in my sleep! No more blog. How would you have coped without it?

That, Jon and Clive, is the reason I couldn't make it to the Wintertones gig last night. I was here at home. Stoned out of my mind!

Perhaps I should have opted for the emergency appointment. The Doctor would probably have found out that I was slowly poisoning myself. Too late now. Never mind. All's well that ends well. As I am sure someone's Granny must have said. I'm going to keep the appointment. There is a mole on the side of my face that I ought to have looked at.

My lottery tickets didn't win, but the Doctors receptionist was right. I am very lucky today.

As a youngster of eleven years old I was

gainfully employed every morning, including Sunday, to deliver newspapers in the neighbourhood I then lived in. Getting out of bed at five thirty every day was difficult for me but I managed it. Albeit with the harsh words, and occasional slap of encouragement from my foster mother ringing in my ears.

Sunday's were particularly awful because the newspapers were twice as big and heavy on that day. The straps of the bag would press painfully into my scrawny shoulders as I plodded my weary way through the streets. Rain, hail, sleet or snow, the papers had to be delivered. Delivered to people who were likely still snug in their warm beds.

How I envied those happy kids on their shiny bicycles that I had seen in American films. They didn't worry about closing gates, or making sure that the paper went all the way through the letterbox. Oh no! All they had to do was toss a folded paper onto the front porch, as they cycled past with a cheery, "Hi Mrs Robinson, thanks for the apple pie. Pop says after Mom, you're the best dang apple pie maker ever."

Those American kids always looked so healthy too. With their freckles, brushed hair and smiling faces. Whereas I probably had the forlorn appearance of a Dickens urchin, with my patched clothes and hob nailed boots, the soles tied on with string.

Despite or maybe because of, my scruffy appearance, I had managed to attract the unwanted attentions of a vile man.

A man I was unable to avoid. He was the caretaker of a block of flats. I had two papers to deliver here. One to him and one to a flat on the top floor, three storeys up.

This man began his predatory attentions towards me by standing in his front doorway wearing nothing but an old dressing gown, undone to display his underwear. I knew instinctively, and despite his friendly smile, that he should not be trusted. The fear inside me clouded my life for weeks on end.

My avoidance strategy was to dash through the communal entranceway, shove the paper as quick as I possibly could into the caretaker's letterbox and then dash upstairs, deliver the next one and dash back down again. Praying all the time that he would not be there waiting for me. He always was.

After a while he dispensed with his underwear and began to appear naked under his dressing gown. He would be standing there exposing himself when I arrived, and take the newspaper from me. He would be there when I came back down the stairs. He would leer and smile, try to engage me in conversation. I would wriggle past him, my heart thumping in my throat, as I escaped.

One day, as I was about to make my usual dash for freedom, he stood in front of me holding a pair of trousers, "These might fit you." he said. Making as though to measure them against me, he grabbed me and... I will spare the details.

Screaming and shouting as loud as I could, "GET OFF ME! LEAVE ME ALONE!" and other words a boy should not know, I forced him to back off, and he scurried back to his flat.

Shaken and in tears I continued on my round. Even if I had someone to confide in, it is very doubtful whether I would have done so. Incidents of this nature were not spoken of in those days. My outraged reaction had its desired effect however. That man, who had caused me to live in fear for weeks on end, did not bother me again.

Move forward a week or two. My foster dad and I are looking down a manhole in the front garden. It is blocked and backed up. Threatening to overflow. Drain rods are needed urgently and we don't have any.

Now please do not ask me how an eleven-year-old boy could be this devious, but I saw a chance for revenge and I took it. "Dad, I know someone who will have drain rods. The caretaker at the flats."

"Do you think he would mind lending me them?"

"No Dad. I deliver his paper every day. D'you want me to ask him?"

"OK, no harm in asking I suppose."

So it was, that I found myself standing nervously at the door of the caretakers flat. Mustering what bravery I could, I knocked robustly.

This was the first time I had seen him fully dressed. He looked different. Smaller somehow. Less scary. He looked about him as he opened the door, "what do you want?"

"My Dad and my big brother are coming to see you." I stood and watched his face turn ashen as the blood drained from it, before I turned and ran away.

We went together my Dad, foster brother, and I, to collect the drain rods. There was a little confusion on everyone's part as to why we were there. But when the penny did drop, the caretaker could not have been more helpful.

Five shillings a week, I earned from that paper round. I bet it cost me that much in shoe leather. Character building experience though!

That's it. OK. Right. I have definitely decided.

Yes, why not? I am going to have a determined look at some dating sites. After yet another night out on my own it is time to take action. I need a cuddle.

There must be a woman somewhere, who would be interested in meeting a short, fat, aged, balding bloke with no money, no prospects, and not a lot of hope. Who said the mental asylum?

Surely there are women out there who are desperate to live the simple life. I bet there are thousands of them clamouring to live in a wooden wagon, built from reclaimed timber. Hmm. Maybe best not to mention the wagon.

I suppose if I do go ahead and join a dating agency, I ought to make them aware that I am perfectly happy with this alternative, frugal, lifestyle, apart from the lack of female company obviously, and am far too old to change my ways, even if I was inclined to do so. Which I am not. Having said that, I suppose a little bit of compromise would be required if things are going to work out.

I wonder if it would be appropriate to mention what a fantastic lover I am. No. Perhaps best to let them find that out for themselves. I said them, obviously I meant her. Freudian slip.

As I sit here, thinking about my chances of meeting the woman of my dreams, it has occurred to me that thus far in my life, I have demonstrated time and again, an abject failure to maintain a long-term relationship of any worth. Although I somehow manage to remain on friendly terms.

In the past I have always entered relationships, expecting them to fail. Not even giving them a chance to grow and flourish. I know why this is. It's because I am unable to believe that anyone would really love me. I've always felt that I don't have much to offer. Which is true. I don't

It's all down to the way we are brought up I think. If you have parents with aspirations, then it follows that some of those aspirations will rub off onto you. My parents only ambitions in life, if indeed they had any, didn't include their children. In fact, it didn't even include each other most of the time. Now there you are you see. I've got myself thinking I'm talking nonsense. Because obviously, I would want my children to do well.

But I must face up to the fact. I have never really pushed myself in life. I've always been quite happy with what I've got. Never hankered after the so called good things in life. Never wanted a big house or a top of the range car. I suppose someone with my attitude to life is going to struggle to meet a woman with expectations of a normal comfortable existence.

Listen to me rambling on. Now where was I? Oh yes, I was talking about dating sites wasn't I? Well thank heavens I allowed myself to get side-tracked. It's given me time to think about it. How lucky I didn't rush into joining one. It's patently obvious that they're not for people like me. Best to knock all that nonsense on the head. Why was I even thinking about it?

Phew! That was a close call!

I might just take a quick look though. Can't do any harm, can it? Besides it's a bit unfair of me to deprive the ladies of such a wonderful opportunity.

I'll let you know how I get on.

Did I mention to you that I was thinking

about joining a dating site? Yes, I must have. I share everything with you. Well I've done it! Girded up all my inner strength and done it. It's true. I am now a member of a dating site. Success is guaranteed on this particular site apparently. Which means sadly, that I am going to be extremely busy juggling dates with all the women who view my profile. I say sadly because obviously, there will not be a lot of time left in which to write.

Lovemaking, in my opinion is something not to be rushed, and I expect to be doing a lot of it soon. My gym membership has been renewed. I intend to be in peak physical condition for every one of the beautiful women who are sure to come lusting after me. After all I do think it is only fair to give equally of my time to the hordes of lonely ladies who once they have viewed my portrait, will come knocking on the wagon door, in a feverish sweat of excited anticipation.

I intend to limit myself at first. Not more than two women each day. Best to build up to things slowly. No need to be greedy. As I say this site does guarantee success. So, there will be lots to choose from.

I am so excited! Just think. Me! About to fulfil the dreams, hopes, and aspirations, of so many lonely ladies.

I have always felt that my unselfish, generous, and modest nature would come in useful one day. Therefore, I dwelt on it a lot, as I was writing my profile notes for the site. Sure to be hard for the ladies to resist.

Hopefully they won't be too disappointed when they arrive, and discover that the picture I have used is not actually me, but one of Clint Eastwood. I'm sure they won't be. After all, if the truth be told I am better looking than him anyway. The only reason I used his photo is because it is of a better quality than I could get on my camera. Besides that, we do both wear hats. Also, I have told a little white lie and said that I am over six foot tall. This shouldn't be too much of a problem though. I am going to explain that I have very short legs for my height.

Okay then. I am going off now to check my inbox. Probably have to delete a few messages without reading them. Wouldn't want to crash the system by letting it get overloaded. They'll come back though. Who could resist me?

When I first started on this article I mentioned that I shared everything with you. That is no longer true I'm afraid. I am a gentleman. Well, maybe not always if you get my drift. But some things must remain a secret. I'll keep you informed of course I will. Just not absolutely everything. Hmm. Better get the bedroom tidied.

I've been told in no uncertain terms not to go back until I've filled this paper bag with fag ends. It's not a small bag either. It is one of those brown paper carrier bags. The type that has string handles. My hands are so cold that I can hardly feel them. Every now and again I stop and press them under my armpits trying to get some warmth back into my fingers.

The wind is determined today. A lazy raw wind. To lazy even to bother to go around my shivering frame. Instead it nips and bites nastily into my skinny frame as I plod through the park, my eyes downcast. Searching the ground for the soggy discarded ends of cigarettes. Fag ends or dog ends as they are colloquially known in these parts.

It is not a good day for this line of work, not many people have bothered to sally forth in the bad weather, and of the fag ends I do see, many have been pulverised into a further state of sogginess by last night's rain. Also, and rather annoyingly for someone engaged in this type of pursuit, filter tip cigarettes are becoming increasingly popular. People tend to smoke them right down until there is no tobacco left. Extremely thoughtless!

If I am to fill the bag I must venture further afield. Out of the park and onto the streets.

This is worse than the park. At least in the park I can go about my task relatively unnoticed. Here in the streets people can see me. I dread any of my school friends seeing what I am up to. But there are plenty of fat dog ends to gather here. Men waiting for their wives outside shop entrances tend to smoke as they stand there. The pub is another good place. I can nip inside sharpish and usually manage to empty a few ashtrays into my bag before anyone notices.

This is one of my weekend chores. My caring foster mother, Aggie Davis needs a good supply of fag ends. She has a small business selling roll up cigarettes to all the lodgers in the house. This is one of several money-making schemes she has, and she likes to involve me to a large degree in all of them. I am a useful source of free labour. Cynically, for someone so young, I sometimes wonder if that is why she fosters me.

Later today, after I have finished collecting, she will send me to the tobacconist shop on the corner. There I will purchase on her behalf, a quarter ounce of Virginia Nosegay tobacco. Ten Wills Woodbine cigarettes and two packets of cigarette rolling papers.

My next noxious task is to peel all the paper from the dog ends, which takes an age to do, until I am able to present her with a good heap of old tobacco. This harvested treasure is then carefully blended with the Virginia Nosegay to hide its unsavoury origins.

Aggie will settle herself comfortably on her favourite chair by the fireside, a constant cigarette stuck to her wet mouth, using her nicotine stained fingers to carefully measure tobacco into her little rolling machine.

This is a good time for me. When she is preoccupied like this it gives me a brief respite from her sharp tongue, and fiery moods.

If the weather is cold I will lay on my bed, cuddled up with Lassie the black Labrador. Without fail on occasions like these, I will try to lose myself in a book. Perhaps an Enid Blyton famous five adventure book, or another favourite,

The Swiss Family Robinson. I love to read. I feel secure there between the pages. Lost in a world of my own.

Later, her task complete, Aggie will give me a cigarette to smoke. It is unwise to refuse this kind gesture.

Quite an auspicious start to my online

dating I feel. Eleven women made contact after reading all about me on the dating site I joined a few days ago. Six of them sent me messages. Mostly about what a wonderful change it was for them to read such a refreshingly truthful self-appraisal. Five of them didn't bother with a message. They preferred the direct approach simply indicating that they would like to meet me. This seemed to me to be a good, though modest, return. I had expected more interest if I'm honest, especially since I had included a photograph.

This initial influx happened within the first few hours of me signing up. How exciting I thought, as I eagerly looked up the profiles of my would be romantic interests.

The thought did occur briefly to me as I read, to wonder how they had reached the conclusion that I had written an honest profile. Because according to some, indeed I would go as far as to say most, of these women, men were, in their opinion, liars, cheats and fly by nights. It does appear that an awful lot of women felt badly let down by the whole online dating scene. I suppose it says a lot about the tenacity of women that they continued in their quest to find the perfect man.

Oh dear! How quickly the desires of this ardent potential suitor began to diminish as I read through the profiles. Perhaps it's just the way I am, but I do not want to be subjected to the lists of requirements which I found these ladies have. It seems to me that for me to have a relationship it is necessary for me to be an absolute paragon of virtue. Something I am blatantly not, and have no wish to be. If I wanted to be saintly I would become a priest. Oops! Bad example, but you know what I mean.

I find these things unnecessary and off putting to say the least. Look! Why not just meet up a few times? Get to know each other like this. Surely this would be more in the natural way of things. Find out if he is the man for you in this way. I realise that time is passing by quickly. But maybe a long-term relationship needs a little time to develop. Let's face it, the type of man who you are so keen to avoid, isn't going to take heed of your needs. He's just going to lie to you anyway.

Bit of a tidy up wouldn't go amiss.

In all the profile pictures the ladies look lovely. Glamorous even. This concerns me. I am such a scruffy person myself. Look at the picture I put onto the site. Honestly, I'm ashamed. Not much to get excited about is there? Haven't even tried. I can look better. I'm told that I scrub up quite well. But unless I'm going somewhere special, I'm just not inclined to bother. I do know this statement does not show me in a good light. But that's who I am. Hey! I just realised. Despite my photo, eleven women did respond. What I am trying to say is that I don't want a glamorous woman. Sophistication frightens me.

I haven't arranged to meet anyone yet. Now that the opportunity has presented itself I seem to have lost my nerve. I can talk the talk but it seems I can't walk the walk. I will get there though. Just takes time. No need to rush these things. Patience ladies, please. It's a virtue you know.

Let me meet Miss ordinary. A woman without pretensions. A woman who is happy with herself. A woman who enjoys the simple life. A woman who...

Oh, my God! What am I saying! How hypocritical am I? This sounds just like a list of requirements!

Bonny, my ginger feline friend woke me abruptly this morning, by jumping onto the bedside cupboard and sending everything flying. It was at precisely 1.58 am that this happened. I didn't get upset. Indeed, I felt kindly disposed towards her. She must have timed her jump to coincide perfectly with my inner body clock. Which today even at such a very early hour, would appear to be set at happy. She meant no harm. What she wanted by her action was my attention. I was happy to oblige, and after some stroking and ear rubbing, combined with suitable words of adoration, she returned, purring contentedly, to her own bed beside the window. Leaving me wide awake.

It was far too soon to get up, and so I lay there for a while thinking. My mind travelling back to my early childhood in a home run by London County Council. Specifically, because my mood was good, I was thinking of people who have had some positive influence on me.

Eventually, the thought occurred to me to get out of bed and write it down.

Which is how I come to be sitting here at four o'clock in the morning, shivering slightly, for the sun, unlike me is not yet up. Perhaps the cold will keep me sharp, and focused on the job in hand. Which is to introduce you to some special people.

People like Mrs Williams, a primary school teacher. A kind and pretty woman with a smiling open face. Mrs Williams looked and smelt delicious. She was fond of wearing tight sweaters, that defined and accentuated her ample breasts perfectly. I adored her. Thinking about it now, she was my first love. Five years old! An early awareness.

Mr Hewitt, was also a primary school teacher. He taught me how to read. Gave me individual attention. Of course, he gave everyone individual attention, but he made me feel special. The mark of a great teacher. I used to wish he was my dad. Mr Hewitt smoked a pipe with great enthusiasm, and spoke, suck puff, slowly, suck puff, and suck puff, thoughtfully, suck puff, like this.

One day there appeared in this residential children's home, a new face. This was Mr Heap, the superintendent. Until he appeared on the scene I hadn't even been aware that there was a home superintendent. I never got to know him well, but a smiling benevolence radiated from him always. Something which meant a lot to me. Sadly, I left the home soon after he arrived, but nevertheless he was a definite influence, simply by the fact that he acknowledged my existence.

I must not forget to mention Miss Steed. She also came into my life shortly before I left the home. She was the new housemother. A kind and loving woman who cared about us all. Her first job was to rid the house of the myriad of notices which were stuck everywhere you looked. Warning notices, don't do this, don't do that, type of notices. Miss Steed thought that such things did not belong in our house. It was good to see them go. She made lots of changes to the formerly strict regime. Life was much happier with Miss Steed. I would likely have been better off staying with her. But the future wasn't mine to decide.

Reg was one of the gatekeepers. I spent long periods in the gatehouse with him as I waited, often in vain for my Mother to visit. On the many occasions when she failed to turn up as expected Reg would hug me and wipe away my tears with his enormous white handkerchief. I'm sure he kept that handkerchief specially for that purpose. I suppose many kids needed a comforting hug at times. Sadly, these days Reg's kindness and hands on approach towards us children would be frowned upon. But he was simply a warm hearted caring man. I liked Reg.

The other gatekeeper was George. He would play snakes and ladders or Ludo with me, as we whiled away the time waiting for mum to arrive. Later on, when I was older, and was allowed to venture outside the grounds of the home I would visit George and his wife at their house across the back field. His lovely wife used to make little sponge cakes with icing on them. A rare treat for a boy in those spartan times just after the war. George once gave me a shilling to buy a white mouse and made me a cage for it. I wasn't allowed to keep it in the home but I left it with George and would visit my mouse whenever I could.

Because my Mother was prone to let me down. I was sometimes visited by Uncle Bob and Auntie Sheila. Not real family but a foster Aunt and Uncle. They had a motorcycle and sidecar. I would be strapped to Uncle Bob on the back of the motorbike, Auntie Sheila in the sidecar and off we would go, for a day out. Nice memories. Sometimes I would spend a weekend with them. Once or twice during school holidays I would spend a whole week or more with them at their house. I loved it, but it had to end because I would get too distressed when it was time to return to the home. I hated leaving them. I can still feel the heartache of it today.

Just before I finish, I must mention someone who I never actually met, but who I admired greatly. I am referring to the wonderful comic actor and film star Norman Wisdom. Every once in a while, there would be a film show held on a Friday evening in the school hall. Norman was making lots of films at that time in the 1950's and so he would often feature at these nights. I loved it. He made me forget all the sadness in my life as I laughed along to the storyline. Maybe I identified with the little man who fought against authority and always came out on top. I didn't analyse it in those days. I just knew it made me happy. Strangely enough when I was older and read his autobiography I discovered that his life had many parallels to mine. Perhaps that is why he could portray pathos so well. Norman Wisdom died recently. I felt the loss. My extremely handsome son George bought me a boxed set of all his films. I still enjoy them.

Well that's it. The sun is just over the horizon. Looks like it will be a nice day. Bonnie has woken again and wants her breakfast. Sadie and I shall take a walk over the fields. After that, I have plenty to keep me busy today. I still feel good. Hope it lasts.

At the end of a very long and exciting overnight journey from London, aboard a train, pulled by the famous 'Flying Scotsman' locomotive, My Mother and I arrived at Aberdeen station. It was 1959 and I was rapidly approaching my 13th birthday.

Up until this time it had been several years since I had seen, or had any contact with my Mum. This estrangement had ended suddenly and without warning just the day before, when she appeared at the door of my current foster parents and told the foster mum that she was taking me.

I can vaguely recall some argument between the two of them as to the legality of such a move. But Mum was determined, and as I was soon to find out, could be ferocious, when she wanted to get her own way. Which was quite a lot of the time.

She had obviously won the argument. Because here we were, in another country, Scotland. The beautiful land of her birth. I was so excited and thrilled to be with her. I am able even today to conjure up the heady sense of release and freedom I felt. The joy of knowing that I was with someone I had yearned to be with for so long. Someone who loved me.

As far as I was concerned all buses were supposed to be red. But here in Aberdeen the bus we boarded was bright yellow. Mum called it a bus, but it didn't have an upper deck. To me it should have been called a coach.

People were talking, holding conversations, but I struggled to understand what they were saying. It might have been a foreign language, except that I could make out the odd word or two. Just these small differences added to the sense of adventure I was experiencing.

I had never seen, or travelled such quiet narrow roads as this before either. If we did encounter traffic, there was hardly room to squeeze two vehicles past each other.

Everywhere I looked there were dry stone walls of grey granite dividing the fields. Fields full of cattle and sheep. Even pigs. Fascinating stuff for a boy from the big city.

Purple heather and yellow gorse and broom on the hilly terrain all added to my feeling of being in a foreign country.

Oh, my word what's that! Mum! Mum! Look it's a mountain! It's a mountain! Well I'd only seen a mountain in films before, this was so exciting, and what's that on top of it. Looks like snow. It is snow! It's the start of the summer holidays and there's snow!

We stop at a village. There are grey granite houses. Pink granite houses. The granite glints and sparkles in the sunshine. Several small shops, with old fashioned painted signs. Lots of people alight here. But we still have a few more miles to go.

Nearly there now. Mum points out a small cluster of granite built houses in the distance and a slight feeling of apprehension takes me. It is almost time to meet Jimmy, her new husband. Everything will be all right though. I'm with my Mum.

Yesterday I was an unhappy child in a foster home in the crowded, bustling smog ridden metropolis of London. Today less than twenty-four hours later, I am breathing the clean sweet air of rural Scotland, and walking up a rutted country track towards a small stone cottage with matching outbuildings.

Swallows are swooping. The sky is blue, and there in the near distance is 'Bennachie'. A real mountain with snow on the top.

I am home, and with my Mum. Will everything be all right? Only time will tell.

Mother and I have completed the long

overnight journey from London, England, and have just
alighted from a bus, having finally arrived at our
destination. A croft, in the shadow of the mountain
Bennachie, about twenty miles distant from Aberdeen in
north east Scotland. I have enjoyed the journey, and wish it
could go on for a bit longer. It has been wonderful being
the focus of my Mums attention. At the same time, I am
excited to know what comes next.

It is 1959. I am twelve years old. Until her sudden
appearance at my foster home yesterday, I had not seen my
Mother for many years. She is almost a stranger. A
stranger I am thrilled to know and love.

On our right-hand side as we lugged our suitcases up the
gently sloping track to the croft house was a well-tended
vegetable garden. Neatly spaced, tidy rows of plants
growing in profuse, well ordered abundance. On the left
were the back walls of the next-door croft house and
outbuildings. All the same ubiquitous grey granite which
also made up all the drystone walls in this region.

The track led to a yard enclosed on two sides by a house
with outbuildings. As we drew near, a flock of what
seemed to be hundreds of chickens but in reality, was
about fifty, came flapping and squawking towards us, and
milled chaotically around our feet, so that I didn't know
where to step next. Mum disappeared into one of the
buildings and reappeared with a pan of corn which she
began to scatter on the ground. All the while screeching
raucously, "Heeeere chick chick chicks. Heeeere chick

chick chicks". This was the first time I had heard anyone calling chickens, and I found it highly amusing. I was also glad that they responded to her calling and left me in peace. Nowadays I use the same call to get my chickens attention at feed times. I notice that my extremely handsome son George has adopted the same call. It is becoming a tradition, perhaps it will go on forever.

It was a kind of relief when I found out that Jimmy, Mum's new husband was not yet home from his work at the local quarry. I don't know why I was apprehensive. Maybe just a boy's shyness. Awkwardness about knowing what to say at a first meeting. But anyway, I was concerned for some reason and was glad to find I could put off the moment.

This also gave me the opportunity to satisfy my curiosity about my new home and environment, and explore unhindered by my innate shyness.

After the journey the need to answer a call of nature was somewhat urgent upon me and I asked my Mother where the toilet was. It was a bit of a surprise when she directed me to a small wooden building at the back of the house. Inside was a plank of wood with a round hole in it. Underneath the plank and aligned with the hole, was a white enamel bucket with a handful of grass in the bottom. This was the primitive toilet. It turned out that this was mainly there for the comfort of visitors. I would soon be expected to take a spade and do my business up the hill, among the gorse bushes. I quickly got used to it.

There was no bathroom. The only place to wash in any degree of comfort was at the stone sink in the kitchen. The water came from a well via a cast iron hand pump. It was always cold and refreshing to drink. This pump had to be primed before each use by pouring a jug of water down it.

There was also a bigger water pump in the yard which was mainly used to fill the cattle trough, but was also where Jimmy had his morning wash. I have no idea where Jimmy had a bath.

My fortnightly scrub was in a tin tub full of lukewarm water in the living room. Not surprisingly this was a bit of an ordeal and I liked to get it over as quickly as I could. Mum had the same routine as me.

The first time I saw Mum taking a bath in this way I felt terribly embarrassed and disconcerted. I had never seen a real live naked woman. She however didn't seem at all concerned by her nudity or the fact that I was in the room, and even used to get me to scrub her back with a flannel. Most times though we would just have a strip wash beside the kitchen sink. This wasn't unusual. Lots of people used this method of personal hygiene in those days. Especially in country areas.

At this stage I want to apologise dear reader. I feel that this post is not well constructed. I am drifting from my intended purpose which was to introduce you in an ordered way to my new home. My chaotic mind is in full flow this evening. However, it will I am quite hopeful, lead to the place I want to take you.

The house was small. Two rooms upstairs and two down. My bedroom was upstairs. The sloping ceiling had a small skylight window on one side, and the room was quite dark. There was no electricity. I would see my way with candles or oil lamp. The bed was old and very high off the floor. Which gave plenty of room for the china chamber pot underneath it. The feather mattress was soft and yielding and would almost engulf my body when I lay down on it. It was really cosy in the winter, especially when I also had a stone hot water bottle beside me.

The other room upstairs was always locked. But a locked door is a source of immense interest. When I did find the key I could not resist a look inside. It was a store room, and contained all the belongings, clothing and photographs of Jimmy's first wife who had died many years before. He had kept everything. I felt like an intruder, and did not look in there again.

Downstairs was the living room. There was a small cooking range here but Mum mainly used a small electric cooker in the kitchen. The socket for this was the only source of electricity in the house. Despite the lack of facilities, she was a fantastic cook and I discovered how good food could be when I lived with her. I had always been a fussy eater in the past. This was probably due to the quality of the food served up.

The kitchen was just a wooden lean to attached to the front of the house. It was also the only way in or out of the house.

The other room downstairs was Mum and Jimmy's bedroom.

It soon became apparent that there was not a lot of marital bliss went on at the other side of that door.

Occasionally, and without knowing why, I am inspired to start painting a picture with only the vaguest of an idea in my mind. Possibly brought about by something from my past. Or seen in a film or on television. Maybe something I have read has triggered an image in my mind. Something seen or read about. Apparently forgotten, but stored untidily in the hidden depths of my memory.

As the idea in my mind grows stronger it gradually reveals its content to me. At this stage I will squeeze a colour onto my palette, thin it down, and using a brush begin to roughly layout my design. This must be done quickly or I will get bogged down in the small details and the image will start to lose its hold on me. I do not allow myself any reference guides once I begin painting. Which explains the somewhat out of perspective size of the baby lambs. I just think a certain naivety adds to the charm. At least that is my excuse and I am sticking to it!

In a short and frantic painting session, I will have mostly completed what I set out to do. Which is to transfer the picture in my head onto a canvas. After a bit of tweaking I will soon know if I have achieved my objective.

This painting, done at the end of last year, and which I present for you to see today, is one of those which pleased me. At least in so far, as the small amount of satisfaction I allow myself to have with my work.

There was a familiarity in this painting, that puzzled me. Had I painted something which had already been done? Had I plagiarized someone else's work?

Eventually the answer struck me. I had painted a portrait of Jimmy, my Mum's new husband. My step-father. The background too is familiar. It is Bennachie! The mountain range, nearby the croft we lived on in Scotland. All totally by chance. A picture painted from inside my head. Very strange feeling this. I absolutely had no idea that I was painting his portrait. But there was no doubt in my mind. Even down to the cap on his head, the finished work was Jimmy Mackie. Crofter, Quarryman, Freemason and amateur wrestler.

A man I liked. A man I hated. A man I came to love and understand in turn. Sadly, this revelation of my feelings towards him came too late. Jimmy was in the terminal stages of cancer when I began to view our relationship in a different light, and knew that he was, under a brusque and hard exterior, an inherently good man.

These days I am honest with my feelings. I will express them openly. Sometimes I am sure, to the embarrassment of the recipient. But if I like someone they will be informed of the fact. If my initial impression of a person is not a good one I give myself time. My instincts have been so wrong in the past. Dismiss someone too soon and you could be losing a potentially good friend.

Here endeth the lesson. One of the benefits of having been around a long time. You can get away with sermonising occasionally. Just don't overdo it!

It's a miserable day outside.

The glorious sunshine we have enjoyed here recently has gone. Which is a shame because it is the school holidays. A good time to go out and draw portraits.

I have to earn some extra money. My car needed work done on it. This is one of those times when the simple life philosophy falls down, and real life takes a bite at you. Why aren't any of life's necessities cheap? Oh well, never mind. There is always tomorrow. I'm expecting blazing sunshine again. After all it is supposed to be flaming June!

Having had such a long spell of nice dry weather only serves to make the rain seem wetter than ever. We need the rain though apparently. Farmers need it for their crops. Gardeners need it for their gardens. Well all right then. In that case, I'm prepared to accept it on their behalf. But just for today! The weeds in my plot are doing very nicely as it is thank you. I'm not inclined to look favourably on anything that might encourage them further.

While I wait for the Sun to make a reappearance I thought this might be a good time to update you on news from the dating site I joined recently. I do know that a few people have asked to be kept informed, and far be it for me to disappoint them.

This site I have joined does guarantee success, so I was not too surprised when the messages began to come in thick and fast. It seems that a lot of women found my profile write up very refreshing in its honesty. How they knew I was being honest, well I haven't figured that out yet. I might easily have been a complete rogue. Instead of the part one I actually am. Oh come on! Nobody is completely perfect. Are they? Anyway, suffice to say I was pleased with the results. Particularly since I had used a less than flattering picture of myself to accompany my refreshingly honest words. Which just goes to show that women do not merely judge a book by its cover. Unless it's a Mills and Boon romance book that is.

I then decided to add another photo showing myself in a better light. You know. Scrubbed up a bit. Beard coiffed. (Coiffed? Where do I conjure these words up from? Excuse me while I look it up, see if I've got it right. Yep! the context is OK. The word does apply to hair at least). Shirt and tie, that sort of thing.

The new photograph produced even more results. It was quite dramatic in fact. Messages from women coming at me from left right and centre. Even several from interested men, wondering if I would be prepared to consider changing my sexual orientation. Obviously, I'm not but I have filed the letters safely away. Just in case I change my mind!

All these lovely ladies wanting to meet up presented me with a big headache. Obviously, being a man of integrity and honour, I don't want to let any of them down or deprive them of this once in a lifetime chance to get to know me.

But I am not just a very handsome, debonair, humble and charismatic man. I have also been blessed with high intelligence. It was not long before the solution to the problem came to me. The answer was simple and I could foresee no problems with it. What I would do to whittle down the numbers into a shortlist was: take the ladies out on a date four at a time. Yes, I know. I thought so too. I am a genius!

Naturally, when the evening ends, there is some competition amongst them about who gets to take me home for, ahem, 'coffee'. But I've sorted that problem out also. I drink a lot of coffee.

I have a confession to make. Those

lovely ladies aren't really my latest dates. The whole thing is a sham. Of course, you probably guessed as much, but just in case any of you thought that the post was true I thought it best to come clean. Besides which I am sure that nobody would believe I could describe myself in such glowing, self-glorifying over the top, terminology. Even if it's true. Would they? Oh dear! Really!

The ladies are all happily married. Their husbands are all just out of shot, keeping a close eye on me, and I can't say I blame them. With my looks and charismatic personality, it is easy to see why they might see me as a threat.

These lovely people are my friends and we are out enjoying an open mic night. For anyone who might be wondering what an open mic night is, it is simply an opportunity for anyone, singers, musicians, poets, comedians etc. to get up and entertain. I, needless to say, am all of the above things. Also, it is a great place for any aspiring young entertainers to learn their trade and hone their acts.

What has happened in this photo is that I have just finished singing and all the women have become besotted with me. Oh, good grief! Here I go again!

Let me try again. The truth this time. No silly flights of fancy. Here goes then. We were all having a lovely time in the pub. I was sitting with the ladies. We were chatting away happily, and even though they are all married they were trying their hardest to get my phone number out of me. No! No! That is not true. I am drifting once more into the realms of fantasy. Forgive me please. I'll get there in the end.

The conversation got around to the dating site I have recently joined. They wanted to know how I was getting on. How many women I had met. Had I met anyone I really liked. Things like that. The upshot was that I said I would tell all about it on my next blog post. That is when the idea came to me for this photograph. I asked them if they would mind looking at me as though they were completely smitten, and they happily went along with it. Actually, it was quite simple. To be honest they were already looking at me adoringly. I have this effect on the ladies. It is something I have had to learn to live with. Life can be so unbelievably cruel sometimes. Oops! Here I go again. Sorry about that.

The truth is that the dating is not going well. Oh, there have been lots of messages from women who would like to meet me, that much is true, and I have responded to a few. But nothing has happened yet. Also, I have not written to any of the women first. I just wait for them to make the initial contact. I don't think that is the way it should be. But it is the way it is. I am nervous of rejection. There has been enough of that in my life. I am a failure.

Oh, that is so sweet of you to disagree and I know you mean well. But it is true. I am a failed date site has been. Or perhaps that should be, hasn't been.

Underneath this happy, confident, 'Jack the lad' exterior is a quiet, shy, and somewhat disillusioned man. Why I ask myself should I want a relationship again, when I have made myself and others so unhappy in the past. Perhaps it would be better if I remained on my own. Where, if I am honest I am quite happy.

Life is simple, uncomplicated. I don't want for anything. I see my extremely handsome Son and his mother when I want to. I have friends. I get out and about. Go places. I have my music. My art. My pets. My freedom.

Why complicate things with a new partner? Of course, I have asked myself this question a hundred times, a thousand times, and still do not know the answer. The best I can come up with is that people are not designed to live alone. We need someone to share the highs and the lows. Perhaps companionship is a basic essential of life. It is an established fact that married people live longer than unmarried. Hey! I just had a thought. Maybe it only seems longer.

God! I've started rambling again. What do I know about life or relationships? Except how to make a mess of it.

Where is Sadie the German Shepherd? My faithful friend. I need a hug. No photographs of this event will be shown. Sadie and I are both terribly shy. Anyway, I don't expect you will ever believe anything I say again. Photograph or not.

It is the early 1950's. I am six or

seven years old, and living in a children's home on the outskirts of London.

Saturday morning. I am perched on a hard-wooden bench, which has been highly polished over the years by the serge trousered bottoms of many a small boy in just the same situation as I am now. This bench is in the waiting room of the lodge house beside the main gate.

My mood as I wait, is one of expectant excitement. I have been in a fever of anticipation for several days. Ever since being told my Mother was coming.

Something is happening. I hear Reg's chair being pushed back from his desk. My tummy has that funny fluttery feeling again. Is it my Mum? Is it? Is she here? The tears are prickling my eyes. I will cry. I know that. But happy tears or sad?

Click, clunk, scrape, snap. Click, clunk, scrape, snap. Click, clunk, scrape, snap. The familiar sound of Reg's artificial leg precedes his appearance at the waiting room door.

"She's here Johnny Boy. She's here. Pick your case up. We don't want to be keeping her waiting now do we?" Reg has a great mound of curly ginger hair and it bounces about with the nodding of his head as he speaks. He is in a fluster of excitement on my behalf.

Too many Saturdays have he and I waited in vain for my Mother to turn up at the arranged time. Too many

Saturdays has he spent consoling me as I sobbed with unhappiness. But not today. Mum is here, and not very late either.

She greets me effusively with a big hug. I like her face with the bright red lipstick. I like her brown wavy hair. I like her coat with the big belt buckle and the soft collar, and I like the way she smells. I would hold on to her forever if I could, if she would let me, but we have to get moving.

After Mum has signed the register book, Reg ruffles my hair and winks at me. "Go on then," he says smiling. "Give it a kick. You won't hurt me." He always does this. It's his favourite joke.

Drawing my foot back I kick out at his wooden leg.

"Ow! Ouch!" he shouts in mock pain, "that's the wrong leg!" Then he laughs and limps back into the gatehouse. I like Reg. His real leg got bitten off and eaten by a Lion at London Zoo, because he got too close and put it through the bars of its cage. All us kids know that.

Off me and Mum go. Laughing and happy. I was right about the tears though. They are there.

Our first stop is the sweet shop. It is the shop where I would normally spend my threepence pocket money. Usually I am in an agony of rushed indecision as how best to spend my pennies, but not today. Consumed with avarice and heady joy, I fill a brown paper bag to the brim with gobstoppers, blackjacks, sherbet dips and liquorice sticks. I can do this because this is my Mum and she says I can.

We sit on the top deck, in the front seats of a red London bus. It is a wonderful place for a young boy to be. I can pretend to be the driver. Or I can just sit and observe the people on the streets as they go about their business. In the sheltered confines of a children's home it is easy to forget the outside world exists at all. Everything is a wonder to me, and my inquisitive eyes struggle to take in the passing scene.

Next there is a long, and sometimes alarming journey on a London underground train. It sways and rattles its way through the dark tunnels. There is nothing to see except the reflection of myself and the other passengers in the dirty windows. Everyone is silent and avoiding eye contact with each other by burying their heads in a newspaper or staring up at the advertisements adorning the carriage walls. It is far too noisy to talk anyway. I try to break the monotony by jumping up and trying to catch hold of a hanging strap. But I am too small, even if I stand on a seat.

It is a relief when we finally reach the end of the line and alight. There is another bus journey, but it is a short one. Mum and I alight at a stop on a quiet country road. We walk for a time and turn into a track leading through a thickly wooded area. Soon the smell of wood smoke fills my nostrils and I see a shelter built among the trees.

I recognise the man who comes to meet us. It is Fergie, Mums friend. He greets us warmly, lifting me up to plant a stubbly, whisky and tobacco scented kiss on my cheek and carrying me towards the shelter. One of half a dozen or so in the woodland clearing.

This rough tent like structure is what is known as a 'bender'. It is constructed from bent hazel and willow branches covered in bracken or whatever is available in the nearby locality. In some cases, it can be finished, like this one of Fergie's with a strong canvas. Inside the bender, it is warm and cosy. A pile of bedding is at the far end. There is a hurricane lamp and candles. This is where Mum lives, and where I will live too for the next idyllic few days.

Outside a large iron pot is hanging, steaming above a blazing campfire. Dinner is almost ready.

I am home.

No doubt about it. We children's home

kids were a God-fearing lot. It was constantly being drummed into us how the Almighty would bring down his wrath upon our unworthy souls should we even think of straying from His righteous path.

Every school day at morning assembly, we would be reminded that the Lord was everywhere. He saw and heard everything we did.

Every mealtime before and after eating, we said a grace, thanking Him for our food.

Every night before we lay down to sleep, we would get onto our knees beside our beds, and pray that He would keep us safe.

Twice a day on Sundays, morning and afternoon, a large, noisy gaggle of well-scrubbed boys and girls, wearing Sunday best clothes and polished shoes, would be formed into a semblance of an orderly line.

On the given command and shepherded by frowning, fussy and urgently cajoling houseparent's, "keep up. Stop talking. Why are you looking behind you? Keep moving. Hold that little one's hand. Your laces, do them up. No! Not there, you stupid child!" We would straggle, hand in hand, and two abreast, through the ornate cast iron gates of the home, and onwards, like little Christian soldiers, to the local Methodist church. A distance of about half a mile. There to be reminded of how wicked and unworthy we all were.

Having yawned and fidgeted our way through the afternoon service, it was then time for us younger kids to attend Sunday school.

Here we would be reminded of how much God loved us. This, even though we had already been told at least twice that day by the Minister, that we would go to hell, and suffer eternal damnation, if we did not obey God's will.

If one of us kids wanted to make it absolutely clear to another kid that what we were saying or about to say, was the total truth, we would always place a hand on our heart and say the words, "Gods honour." These two words were always said with profound piety, and great seriousness, and would never be taken lightly.

We children knew that lying, cheating, and stealing were wrong, and would not be tolerated. On the rare occasions that an act of this nature did occur, it was punished severely by the teachers or houseparent. But worse still, the rest of us knew that God would be extremely angry.

We impressionable youngsters truly believed this to be an indisputable fact. That is the measure with which I say, that we children's home kids were, without doubt, a God-fearing lot.

Aggie Davis, the new foster mother with whom I have been recently placed, is teaching me how to steal from shops. Stealing is wrong. This has been ingrained into me my whole life. I am fearful. I know God will punish me. But I am scared of Aggie. Her temper is fearsome. She beats me. Punches, kicks, and pinches me. I will do what she tells me to do. Hopefully God will understand.

Hi, Sadie the German Shepherd here again.

He's been reading that newspaper for long enough now. I intend to sit here with my head resting on his knee and looking at him with my big soulful eyes until he puts the paper down, and notices me.... Alright then this is not working. I shall poke my nose up under the paper and give it a bit of a nudge.

"SADIE! Oh, for God's sake. Now look what you've done."

Not my fault. How was I supposed to know he had a mug of tea in his hand? I'll lick it off the floor. Save him a job.

He's still tetchy. No need to glare at me John. I'll lie down and put my paws over my eyes. That'll calm him down a bit. I really don't know why he shouts at me. It only makes him feel guilty.

What's he eating? Is it a doughnut? It is a doughnut. I'm entitled to a bit of doughnut after being shouted at like that. I'll try the German Shepherd whine, big soulful eyes combination. Never fails.

"No Sadie! Go away. You are not having any. It's not good for you."

Not good for me. What a nerve he's got. He has just eaten three jam doughnuts with sugar on and he says they're not good for me. Oh, but I suppose eating jam doughnuts for breakfast is good for you, is it Mr health conscious? What happened to the oatmeal and blueberries you're always telling everyone you have for breakfast? Alright then if you are going to continue to behave so selfishly I will go and eat the cat's food.

Well that got his attention. Now I shall have to listen while he tells me I will not be getting any dinner this evening. Because I am just a greedy dog who has no respect for Bonnie's needs. He's right there. I haven't.

"Right! No dinner for you tonight. You are so greedy Sadie. No! Don't give me the hangdog look. What is Bonnie going to eat now eh?"

That cat gets far too much attention if you ask me. Besides, if she leaves food in her dish what does she expect?

He's putting his boots on. This looks promising. Could be a walk. I'll try a little bit of a hopeful whine.

"Shut up Sadie. You're not my friend."

Hmm. Still a bit grumpy then. I'll try the waving a paw routine. See if I can jolt him out of it.

"What are you doing now? Gimme a paw then. Come on shake hands. Clever girl."

That's better. Works every time. Now hurry up and tie those bootlaces. In case you have forgotten we didn't have a walk yesterday because of continuous heavy rain. I have a lot of catching up to do.

"Where's your lead Sadie? Find it. Find your lead."

Why do we always have to go through the find your lead rigmarole. He knows perfectly well that I tend to get over excited at walk time. Next thing you know he will be telling me to calm down.

"CALM DOWN SADIE!"

What did I tell you? It's the same every time.

"Sadie. Come. Sit."

No, I am not going to sit. Sorry.

"Saaadieee. Sit."

I'm not going to sit.

"Saaadieee. SIT!"

John. In case you have not noticed. We are standing in a big puddle of muddy water. Would you sit in it? No, you wouldn't. Well, not unless you had just got back from the pub. But perhaps best not to mention that incident.

"Sadie Down."

Now he is being ridiculous. Give him time.

Did the day start off all right weather-wise? I
ask myself the question because it seems such a long time
ago. Yes, it did. I remember now. It was the sun shining
through the mollicroft window that woke me. Looking out
I could see that grey skies were looming. So, decided to
take a quick walk to the village with Sadie the German
Shepherd, before the heavens opened.

Didn't quite go as planned though. Halfway across the
potato field footpath it began to rain. Shall I turn back?
No! It will stop soon. My decision-making skills were in
short supply today. I carried on. It began to pour. By the
time I had reached the other side of the field, the footpath

was a quagmire and I, wearing just a jumper and jeans was soaked through.

At this stage I decided to turn back. Another wrong decision. After just a few yards my boots were heavy with clinging mud, and just got heavier and heavier as I plodded homeward. I should have walked home on the pavement.

The torrential downpour beating on my head and the fact that I do not have windscreen wipers on my glasses, made me keep my head down. Which is the reason I did not see that Sadie had come to a halt on the path. Which is the reason I fell over her. Which is the reason I ended face down in a bunch of angry stinging nettles, and one of my outstretched arms was up to the elbow in a muddy waterlogged rabbit burrow. Of course, it was the arm on which I was wearing my newly repaired watch that ended up in the hole. Not to worry. I never really liked that watch anyway.

With a good supply of the potato field attached to my boots I managed to drag myself home. This wagon of mine does not have the luxury of a porch where I could get out of my wet clothing, and being reluctant to make a mess indoors I removed my muddy boots and sodden clothes outside my door.

Unfortunately, in my haste to divest myself of the wet garments I had forgotten that my door key was hanging in the tractor shed, at the other side of the paddock. I make a naked dash across the grass to retrieve it. The key is not there. I am cold, wet, naked and miserable. It is an effort to think straight. Where is my key. Suddenly I remember. It must be in the pocket of my jeans. Which are now in a wet heap outside the wagon door. I hurry back to the wagon.

Have you ever tried to get a key out of the pocket of a wet pair of jeans? It is very difficult. Especially if you are naked in the pouring rain, with cold hands and bursting to have a pee, and with the added distraction of an excited, and wet German Shepherd dog, thinking that all the naked to and fro rigmarole is some bizarre game you have just invented.

Can you imagine what it must have looked like, a naked wet and shivering man well past his prime, scampering about in a field with his dog? Can you imagine it? Of course you can. I have just painted a picture in your head. I do apologise. It must be horrendous for you. Let me move swiftly on.

Indoors at last, I find the floor is awash. There is a leak in the wagon roof. I feel justified in letting rip with a few choice phrases of the kind you are unlikely to hear in Church. Swiftly I grab a pile of old newspapers and spread them over the floor to soak up the water. While this is going on I am giving myself a vigorous rub down with a towel trying to get the circulation back into my frozen limbs.

Dry clothes and a good deal of mopping up later. I sit down with a nice hot cup of tea and a toasted bacon sandwich.

Oh look! The sun is out again. The sky is clearing. Why the hell didn't I wait? Flaming June? Flaming bloody joke. That's what it is.

Apart from all that nonsense it was not a bad day. I made some money by painting this portrait of a border collie. I thought you might like to see it.

I did my good deed for the day by rescuing a frightened green woodpecker from an equally frightened woman's kitchen. No, I'm afraid I don't know why it flew into her kitchen. But it was marvellous to hold such a bird in my hands for a few seconds. I just wish I had my camera with me. Not just to show you the woodpecker, but the woman screaming. She is frightened of birds. A common phobia I believe.

I wonder what the weather will be like today. If it looks like it might rain. I will not be going out for a walk. Besides, my boots are still wet.

Seventeen years ago, my somewhat

humdrum, stick in the mud, sort of life became transformed, when, Tricia, my partner, to the accompaniment of 'The Beach Boys' singing 'Good Vibrations', gave birth to our son, George.

They were not actually in the room with us. The 'Beach Boys' I mean. No, they had to stay in the corridor outside. Sorry. I am being silly. They were on the radio. Anyway, I remember thinking as I watched my son being born. Urrgghh! Sorry again. I remember thinking that 'Good Vibrations was a great tune to be born to.

There was a lot of screaming and shoving going on in the labour room. But eventually the nursing staff, let me out.

Nine months earlier both Tricia and myself had been somewhat taken aback to find out that she was pregnant. We were in our mid to late forties at the time and to be honest we both thought that our child rearing days were well behind us.

We had of course been responsible adults, and taken sensible precautions against such an event happening. Well, I say we. I should perhaps say Tricia had taken precautions. Her main one being to keep me locked out of the bedroom. All I can think of by way of explaining her pregnancy, is the time we both got hungry in the middle of the night and met unexpectedly in the kitchen. Where she, in a moment of reckless abandonment, suddenly realised what she had been denying herself, and despite my vigorous protests, took advantage of my kind and generous nature. Several times.

It has been wonderful these last seventeen years, watching my extremely handsome son grow up. He started playing football at a very young age, and I have so enjoyed watching him play. He is good enough to have won lots of medals and trophies over the years. I have watched him win best player award at several football camps. One of my favourite football memories was watching him score a goal on the pitch at Goodison Park, home of Everton football club in Liverpool. A club of which George's great Grandfather on his Mother's side, was one of the founding members and which we staunchly support.

He also has a great interest in wildlife, flora and fauna, and we have enjoyed finding out lots of things together on our nature walks and wild camping trips. We both enjoy bush craft. There is not much to beat building a basic shelter in the woods with your son, and cooking over a campfire.

These activities are becoming less as he builds new friendships and starts his journey into adulthood. This is probably just as well for me. I am getting older too. I am ready to lead a more sedate lifestyle. Not too sedate though. I am not ready to give up just yet. There is still a lot of life left in this old dog. But I am pleased that I have been able to be a hands-on type of Dad. I know men younger than me who find Fatherhood exhausting.

George gave me a new lease of life. At forty-six I think it is fair to say that a lot of men begin to think about taking things a bit easier. I began to live again. I am so glad that I had the opportunity to do so.

Although Tricia and I are no longer partners, we are still the very best of friends, there for one another, and still see each other every day. I will always be grateful to her for the gift of our son.

What's brought on all this introspection, you may be wondering? It was Father's Day. My son bought me Sunday lunch. It was delicious.

He also made a great sacrifice for me. At a time when he could have been out with his pals, he came and watched his Dad perform at the open mic night. It must have been hell for him. But he didn't flinch from it. Once again, he made his old Dad proud.

Yes. It has been a wonderful seventeen years. Here's to the next seventeen. But I will not be visiting the kitchen in the wee small hours again. Cheers!

Thinking about what kind of personality I had as a child, I suppose the description that springs to mind would be, a quiet boy, usually somewhat timid, but with a spark of temper at times, a bit of a loner, and eager to please.

Indeed, I am fairly sure that if I could gain access to my files from the council children's home where I spent most of my formative years, those would be the among the words in it.

Children in those days, I'm going back to the early 1950's in my case, were not empowered in the way that modern children are. We were truly, in the words of the old adage, expected to be seen and not heard.

Personally, I was happy to keep my head down. To stay below the radar. Of course, in this case, I am referring to kids who did not have the strength of a loving family around them.

Occasionally though, on those rare times when my Mother would visit, I could experience for myself, the strength which love can bring to a child. My Mothers presence brought with it a sense of security, both mental and physical, which I never felt at any other time. This safe feeling would reveal itself within me by a sense of self awareness. Naturally happiness was a great part of it, but I remember too, that in my Mothers presence I acquired a boldness, a self-confidence, a cheekiness. Feelings normally alien to me, but which, because I felt safe in her love would come to the surface.

Looking back on it now I realise that I was perhaps, exploring the boundaries of just how far I could go. How much would my Mother put up with before she exerted her authority over me.

I can tell you it was a lot further than the staff in the children's home allowed. Egos were not encouraged. We kids were all just part of the greater mass. It was therefore a delicious feeling to be allowed to be myself. Even if it was just for a few hours and on too few occasions.

When Mum said her goodbyes to me, at the gatehouse of the home, I would quickly revert to the quiet timid persona which was my other, more usual, self. Or was it?

Let us travel forward a few years to 1958. I am now in a foster home in London. Eleven years old. A small child for my age. A quiet boy, timid even. The old saying 'he would not say boo to a goose' could fairly be applied to me.

This day I am unwell. Or perhaps I do not want to go to school. Whichever it is. My desire to stay in bed causes a terrible rage to come upon my foster mother, Aggie Davis.

I know what is about to happen. It is a common occurrence. The blankets are pulled from me. I curl myself into the foetal position and she begins her onslaught. I am pulled onto the floor, she screams incoherently, kicking hard into my ribs. She kneels on me heavily, her knees on my chest, as she punches, slaps, and pinches, releasing her full spitting ugly fury on me. Fortunately for me, this witch, this harridan, is unhealthy in body as well as mind, and, is soon too breathless to continue.

But Aggie is not quite finished. She has a parting shot. A practiced routine. She grabs my private parts and twists and squeezes with all her remaining strength, until I scream in agony. This is the only way she can make me cry. They are tears of shame as well as pain.

As I plod my way to school, I take the threepenny coin she always gives me after an assault and hurl it over the fence into the park. I don't want her money. She cannot buy my forgiveness this time.

This is a momentous day. I determine to fight back the very next time she attacks me. I feel my Mothers strength within me. I feel emboldened. Empowered. My determination grows.

The next attack is not long in coming. I have returned from an errand to the local shop with the wrong amount of change. It is a shilling short. Aggie is furious. Accuses me of stealing it. She delivers a painful stinging blow to my head.

I punch out with all my small power, and land a blow on her. She staggers back, holding her beak like nose, and I see blood issuing through her fingers. It is enough for me. I take to my heels like a frightened rabbit.

My welfare officer later finds me sitting on a bench in the local park. He does not ask me about the incident, and I do not tell him my side of it. He has obviously listened to Aggie's version of events, and that will do him. As I say, in those day's children were expected to be seen and not heard.

Eventually I am returned to Aggie's care. My retaliation is never mentioned. She never hits me again. I had achieved the desired effect.

Soon after this incident I leave the foster home for good, when I am reunited with my Mother.

It is the beginning of a slippery slope for me. I will never allow myself to be bullied or beaten again. I am a different boy now. Still quiet. But no longer timid. This will be a new beginning. I am stubbornly determined about that. Trouble is looming for me. Aggie Davis should take her share of the blame.

Why am I doing this? Writing all this

down I mean. It is in part for myself. Here I can rabbit on about my life in a way that people can take or leave. I am doing it for you too, dear reader, because I like to share my story.

Mostly though, I am doing it so that there is a record of my life for my children. Otherwise when I am gone, what will there be left of my existence, apart from a few hazy soon forgotten memories? Oh yes, and a few mediocre paintings.

I have told you some tales from my childhood. About the people, I knew then. Some of them kindly and some of them horrid. At times, it feels to me that I dwell too much on the nastier side of people's characters. Let me tell you that I met a lot of decent people too.

In the turbulent ocean of my somewhat fractured childhood I was fortunate enough at times to find calmer waters and sunnier shores.

Unfortunately, the stormy times are the ones that dominate my memory. Which I suppose is not surprising, since the bad things are the ones that affected me most. How lucky I am that I have a strong survival instinct.

Apart from a short breakdown in my mental health during my thirties, which I spoke about previously and which I attribute to childhood trauma, I think I emerged from being an abandoned child, relatively sound mentally. Though I should say, not everyone would agree with me on this.

However, I went off the rails with a vengeance during my teens and into my early twenties. The chip on my shoulder was more the size of a tree. Fighting and drinking, tore my life apart. Disrespect was my watchword, both to others and to myself.

Merchant Navy training. Fit as a fiddle and well behaved.

Let me stop at this point, my dear readers, and ask you, have you formed an opinion of me, based on the stories I have related thus far? If you have I hope it is a good one. Look at the photo of me in my Merchant Navy uniform. Do I look like a bad boy? Yet I had already been in lots of trouble at this time. I don't really think I was bad. Perhaps troubled would be a more suitable word.

Friends would tell you I am a good man. Kind hearted, generous, loving, a good father. An emotional, sentimental, heart on sleeve type of guy. Yes, they would. I have asked them.

I tell you these good things about myself, so that when I mention, somewhat casually, that I have spent time in prison, you will base any judgement you might make, on the person I am today, rather than the immature, broken youth, I once was. Let me add that my crimes although warranting punishment, were all to do with a massive inferiority complex, which, combined with a serious alcohol intake, refused to let me back down from confrontation. The resulting skirmishes must have been my fault. Everything was my fault in those days. Also, I was involved with a tough bunch of hard drinking 'friends'.

The courts did take my troubled childhood into account when sentencing me, and I was given a lot of chances and professional help to get me back on the right path. But I would not, or could not, learn, and finally the Sheriff, Lord Hamilton, in the high court of Aberdeen, who had got to know me well, decided that I needed a harsh lesson and packed me off to prison.

Did I learn anything from my prison sentence? Yes, I did. Unfortunately, most of what I learned was about how to be a real criminal. But I also learned that I did not enjoy incarceration.

I was still in the merchant navy and on my release, went back to sea. Where, if you will forgive an unintended pun, I began to get my life back onto an even keel. Almost.

Whether in the prison, going to sea, working ashore or travelling around the country with my Mother and her on and off paramour Fergie. My life was once full of adventure.

Do you still like me? I do hope so. If you do, please stay here with me, and I will do my best to keep you interested.

A Complaint by Sadie Bain.

As you know I am of the German Shepherd persuasion. A noble and well respected breed, I hope you will agree.

I did not have a great start in life. A bit like John really. We were both in 'homes' in the early part of our lives. Both of us were quite badly treated. I was a nervous wreck when I first came to work for John, highly strung. Jumped a lot at my own shadow. That sort of thing. It took a long time for us to trust each other. But now I enjoy my work as his companion and protector and love him to bits.

To tell the truth I no longer think about it as work. He's more of a friend these days. In truth, I do get a little possessive at times, although not in a bad way. Unless I sense he is in danger that is. Then I have been known to adopt the full on German Shepherd, get away from my buddy routine.

Please don't spread it about, but that old saying about bark being worse than bite, could easily be applied to me. Strangers don't realise this though, so I can see anyone off with just a bit of noisy role play. Quite an easy job really and as I say, I enjoy my life caring for him.

The food is good, when he has a bit of spare cash that is. No. Let me revise that statement. The food is cheap, but acceptable.

Some unthinking person, once told John that high protein dog food is not good for German Shepherds. Some nonsense about it affecting our back legs. Of course, John saw this as a great chance to save a bit of money and so, as I say, cheap but acceptable.

Ironically, if anything, it's John's legs that are showing signs of wear and tear, not mine. I haven't seen any signs of him cutting back on his rations though. Not that I would want him to because he does throw the occasional piece of steak my way. Anyway, as I say, life is good with John. He wouldn't win employer of the year maybe, But I can't complain.

Until now, that is! I am not too happy with him just now. I feel let down. I have given him years of devotion, and now this has happened.

There is a new kid on the block. A puppy! A cutesy, wootsy, puppy wuppie. Not even a proper dog. It's a terrier. Three times that puppy has visited. Three times!

One ray of hope for me is that it is not John's pup. No, it belongs to his ex, Tricia, who lives next door. She already has two terriers, but they aren't allowed up here because they like to kill hens as a hobby. Tricia thinks it is a good idea to introduce 'Dixie' to the hens. So, she can "get used to them". I suppose that means she's going to be a regular visitor. Huh!

Hallo! I live here too you know. A little consultation would have been nice. Not to mention polite.

I must be on my best behaviour of course. John knows I wouldn't hurt the pup, but Tricia is a nervous wreck every time she sees me with the puppy's head in my mouth. I can't imagine why.

Dixie had better behave herself. I'm the top dog around here. My trouble is I'm too good natured. I mean I am aware that all I have to do is give one quick snap and Tricia would not bring that little pain back here in a hurry.

But no I am a German Shepherd. A noble breed. It won't take me long to show the little upstart who's in charge.

Besides, Tricia has promised me a nice big marrow bone if I'm good.

We are up and about early today Jimmy and me.

I am hoping that he might show me how to *guddle a trout, or, even better, a salmon. Jimmy is my new stepdad, having married my Mother just a few weeks earlier.

The year is 1957. It is the start of the school summer holidays. I am 12 years old. Until just a few days ago, I was living in London, England, and was a real city boy.

I had not seen my mum for a good few years, until she appeared suddenly, and without prior warning, at my foster home, and whisked me off to live the life of a country boy, in the land of her birth, Scotland.

It was the start of a completely new way of life for me, and for her, - this was the first settled home she'd had for many years - and for Jimmy her new husband. My apprehension about meeting him for the first time, was unwarranted, and my relationship with this dour, scar faced Scot, a man of very few words, has developed thus far, into that of acquaintances rather than friends.

As we skirted the fields of the neighbouring farm on our way to the river, Jimmy, shotgun cocked, was ever vigilant for game. It was not long before his little dog Scamp, disturbed a hare from its sett, and said hare was quickly and expertly dispatched with one shot. Before being hidden beside a drystone *dyke, to be picked up on our homeward journey.

Scamp the dog, was a very scruffy black and white mongrel. With bad teeth and malodorous breath. A small, runt like, specimen of a collie. He had only recently acquired the name Scamp from my Mother. Jimmy, although he had owned the dog for about ten years had never seen the point of naming him. The poor little dog probably thought its name was *'awa' tae me' or *'bugger aff'. Scamps rotten teeth and small size, were mainly down to the fact that his usual diet was bread and milk. With the occasional treat of the guts of whichever animal Jimmy had just shot, thrown to him.

To a city lad like me, who had only ever seen the mighty Thames river in London, the banks of the river Don in Aberdeenshire, were a wondrous place to be.

Rippling, tumbling, and sparkling, in one place, and then smooth as glass in another. Deep and dangerous here, and shallow enough to walk across there. Scattered granite rocks and boulders, tempted a young boy to hop from one to another. The occasional slip, and boot full of freezing water, a small price to pay for such joy. Islands of shingle were home to plovers, terns, and oyster catchers. Birds I had only ever seen illustrated in books, were here to see in abundant real life, and did not seem too concerned with the presence of humans.

This was a work day and it was soon time to head home. Jimmy worked at the local quarry, which was the place where he had acquired his scarred face, the result of a tragic accident that had taken the lives of several of his friends. The quarry, from which the granite to build the Thames embankment in far off London had come, was a five-mile bike ride away from home. A ride he undertook in all weathers, and believe me the weather was often extreme in those parts. Mum told me, that apart from the war years, when he served in the army, he had never been late or missed a day in 40 years.

As we made our way back, we were forced into single file on a particularly narrow bit of bank. Suddenly Jimmy stopped, and signalled me to do the same, saying, *"haud on loon." Motioning me to stay low, he removed his jacket and rolled up the right-hand sleeve of his shirt.

After looking along the bank in both directions, to ensure we were not being observed, he slowly and deliberately lay down on the bank. Carefully, he began to dip his hand into the water, until his arm was submerged up to the armpit. Holding tightly to Scamps collar I watched as Jimmy lay there, apparently motionless, for several minutes.

Suddenly, there was a terrific commotion, and thrashing and splashing, in the water. Jimmy rolled his body away from the bank edge, bringing his arm out of the water in a sweeping arc, and in his hand, he held, clamped through its gills, a large struggling, silver flashing, fish. Which he threw backwards over his prone body onto the grass.

"Is it a salmon," I asked excitedly, as I watched Jimmy take a rock, and give the gasping fish, a knock on the head.

*"Aye laddie, richt eneuch," he answered. It was one of the few times I ever saw him smile. *"Dinna tell a'body."

guddle: catch a fish by tickling it.

dyke: wall.

awa' tae me: come here.

bugger aff: go away.

haud on loon: stay there boy.

Aye laddie, richt eneuch: Yes, right enough.

Dinna tell a'body: Don't tell anyone.

Maybe I had been spoilt by the fact that up to now my life at sea had been spent on a BP oil tanker. BP knew how to keep the crew happy. Good food, with a choice of menu, a cabin to myself, and there was even a swimming pool! All heady stuff to a young boy just out of the spartan surroundings of the Merchant Navy Training School at Sharpness, in Gloucestershire.

So, when I first set eyes on my next ship as she stood alongside the quay in Tilbury docks, I did not feel the usual excitement at the prospect of joining her as crew.

I was looking at a tramp steamer. A ship with no redeeming features that I could see. She was in dire need of a new coat of paint, and she was filthy. Colloquially, and justifiably in her case, known as a rust bucket.

Once on board, my pessimistic view of her was not improved. She seemed unloved, untidy and lacked the welcome I normally felt on ships. She made an impression on me, this old girl, but it was not a good one.

The oil tanker captain inspected the crew's quarters once a week, and everywhere on board was clean and tidy. The crew were kept busy on their watches and off watch could relax in pleasant surroundings.

This new berth of mine looked like it had never had a Captains inspection in its entire long life. She was dingy, cramped, and claustrophobic. With four to a cabin. The Bosun was permanently drunk on strong rum. Not much wonder that the ship was in such a sad state.

Sometimes when writing about my young life I have to stop and check my train of thought. Like right now, as I write this, I'm thinking, did I have this thought then, or has this thought just occurred to me? But no. I think I am confident that my feeling at the time was: I am not going to enjoy this ship. My negative vibes were right.

As the cabin boy I was the lowliest member of her crew, and in my opinion the most put upon. Although I should be honest and say, perhaps I only felt put upon because I was a typical teenager.

However, there were two nasty characters on board who seemed to enjoy making my life miserable. They were bullies, and when they were not complaining about conditions on board, filled their off-duty time by playing childish pranks on me and incessant verbal abuse. Banter is normal interaction, and is something that is to be expected on ship. I could deal with banter, and enjoyed it. Nothing wrong with a bit of verbal duelling. If it is kept as fun. Most people know not to go too far with it, and when it is time to back off. Not these two though.

Isn't it strange that nasty people always manage to find each other? What attracted these two morons to each other, apart from their obvious lack of common sense or intelligence, was probably the fact that they were unestablished deckhands. Which means that they had not been through the proper seamanship training. In effect, they were cheap labour. They were not widely accepted or admired by other crew members. Perhaps that was their problem. No sense of self-worth.

I had learned over a tough childhood how to cope with physical abuse but the verbal stuff was something else and I hadn't learned to cope with it. I wasn't able to escape from it either. These two morons were constantly riling and baiting me. Because of my stubborn refusal to back down from confrontation. I was continually trying to give as good as I got from them. But this just played into their hands and only served to spur them on to torment me more. On many occasions on this voyage, because I could not contain my temper, they could reduce me to tears of rage. This of course, dented my fragile pride further and made me feel even worse. Which greatly increased their pleasure.

Isn't it wonderful, how, just when you are feeling that life is miserable, and can't possibly get any worse, that it decides to throw you a lifeline. A welcome gift, an unexpected pleasant surprise, a bonus prize.

Ashore in Greece, things are a bit tense on the streets. I don't know what is happening. This is the 1960's. Perhaps it is the time of the Generals. Whatever the cause, at that time there is friction in the country.

It is a good idea for foreigners to keep their heads down. Which is just what sensible people do. Fortunately for me, my two bullies are singularly lacking in common sense. They think it is clever to distribute leaflets which criticise the government of the day. Obviously, a government sensitive to criticism. A government in a bad mood. The two morons are arrested and thrown into jail.

I have not experienced the inside of a Greek prison, but I am told it is an extremely unpleasant place to be. Dirty and smelly, and apparently, the jailers can be quite violent. Especially to foreigners who distribute nasty lies about their country.

My tormentors never made it back to the ship. The journey back home was much more pleasant. In fact, I think I might even have enjoyed it.

It was so nice being able to politely decline the Bosuns offer to stay on as crew. I was pleased to finally leave the unhappy ship, disembark for good and leave her back at Tilbury.

It was even nicer when I later read in a newspaper, that the morons had each been sentenced to two year's imprisonment in Greece.

I do hope it was not too difficult for them.

A few days ago, I hurt my back while lifting a rocking chair I had made from sticks. As I was lifting it I remember thinking to myself, 'this is a bit heavy, perhaps I ought to get help'.

Unfortunately, as it quite usual with me, being the independent type of man that I am, I did not heed my own advice.

The result is lower back pain. The pain is so bad that I have resorted to taking painkillers. Namely Ibuprofen.

Because I don't take tablets as a rule, their effect on me is quite fast when I do. That's why I forgot about my bad back when I had to push my heavy, and malfunctioning, garden tractor down the drive and onto a trailer.

As the painkiller wore off, I felt the results of this act of stupidity when the pain returned with a vengeance.

My answer was to take a double dose of the Ibuprofen. They are very good, and the pain went very quickly. Which is why I forgot about my bad back when I made the decision that I could no longer bear the sight of all the giant weeds, thistles, nettles and docks which have taken advantage of the mowers recent breakdown and subsequent lack of action.

My solution to this problem was to take the strimmer to the paddock and spend a couple of hours at war against the invaders. Of course, as the painkillers wore off I began to regret this impulsive display of horticultural frenzy and my poor back regretted it even more.

Luckily I still had some Ibuprofen left and three tablets later my back pain had subsided sufficiently enough for me to be caught off guard when my dear friend Elizabeth phoned and asked if I could come over, and lift and move some paving slabs for her. Of course, I was only too pleased to help. Elizabeth always provides a very nice lunch, and, in line with my simple and frugal lifestyle, I hate to miss out on a free meal. Well to be honest I never know when I might eat again.

Oh! Perhaps I ought to mention that my large tummy is because of my genes, and nothing whatsoever to do with over eating. That is the truth!

The pills were rapidly wearing off when I had finished at Elizabeth's and my back reminded me of its fragile condition. Causing me to let out a groan of pain as I slowly and carefully climbed into my truck.

Elizabeth who was about to wave me goodbye was concerned, "oh you poor dear," she said. "Would you like me to give you a back rub?"

"Oh, yes please. Shall I go and lie on your bed?" I answered hopefully, as I jumped, gazelle like, from the truck.

No such luck. She had me lean against the kitchen counter while she massaged some foul-smelling unguent into the small of my back. The result is that I not only have a bad back but I smell like a horse.

I don't have the option of more pills. I daren't take four. That would be silly, and one pill would be just a waste of time now. So, I suppose I shall just have to suffer until my back rights its self. Which hopefully will be soon. Just as long as I remember not to take any more pain killers.

Ibuprofen are marvellous though. Is Ibuprofen a brand name? Do you think they might pay me, if I say it often enough?

The moral of all this is: if you make a rocking chair. Just sit in it!

How long does a person have to live before they are qualified to be known by the prefix 'old'? A long, long time I would think.

Years ago, actually it would have been 1960, when I was a boy of thirteen, and living in Scotland, I had a lovely friend. Everyone referred to her as 'Old Nurse Reid'. I have no idea just how old she was but to my young eyes, and despite the twinkle in hers, she looked ancient. She had served as a nurse in the first world war. So, in the 60's she had certainly been around for a while.

Old Nurse Reid's hair was short, straight, pure white, and brushed back in the no nonsense kind of way, that seemed in those days to be the badge of the professional woman. Her face had a happy plumpness about it. She shone with that rare look, which made you want to confide in her.

Despite having retired from the position many years before, she was nearly always to be seen in the uniform of the District Nurse. Which in those days was a job that carried authority, and great respect. She must have had a good supply of those uniforms because she always had a freshly starched look about her.

By the age of thirteen I had just about given up on school. I was always sent off on time in the mornings but sometime between leaving the house and reaching the school yard I would somehow or other manage to get side-tracked. Often it would be in the company of my friend Doddy, another inveterate truant.

On these occasions, we would spend the day fishing or shooting things with air rifles or catapults, or collecting bird's eggs or butterflies. Anyway, whatever we got up to, it generally involved some carnage to wildlife. Thank God that most of today's youngsters are taught to respect nature. In my childhood, we were nowhere near as aware.

It was on the day's when I was on my own, that I would find myself gravitating to the area of Old Nurse Reid's house. Where I would hang around idling the time away, in the way that only kids can. Climbing trees, balancing on walls, scratching rude words into any surface susceptible to my penknife, seeing if it would be possible to hit that greenhouse with this stone. Oops! Sometimes it was. All those kinds of things which I see kids doing today and frown disapprovingly at, before remembering that I was young once.

Eventually Old Nurse Reid would see me loitering by her gate and invite me in. Which was what I had been waiting for. The usual routine on these occasions was for me to be given a broom and asked to sweep the path or maybe take a wet chamois leather and a bucket of water with vinegar in it, and give her kitchen window a clean. I loved doing odd jobs for her. Strangely I had entirely the opposite reaction when asked to do a chore at home.

When I had completed my tasks, Old Nurse Reid would bring out the cake tin and we would share a slice or two and a cup of tea, while she told me stories about her life, and listened to me complaining about mine. After a while she would ask me to fetch two glasses from the polished oak sideboard, whilst she fetched a bottle of her homemade rhubarb wine from the larder. It was so nice to sit at the table in her cosy little parlour sampling the wine and looking at her collection of photo albums. Where every picture was brought to life by her powers of memory and description.

The rhubarb wine was potent stuff and she would limit my consumption of it, but not before the alcohol had reached my brain and bathed me in its warm glow.

Today Old Nurse Reid would no doubt be castigated for giving alcoholic drink to a child. Indeed, I don't think I would be pleased to hear that my children had been given any, but I liked her and felt good in her company. I like to think that she felt the same about me.

Looking back now there was a conspiratorial air to our little wine sampling sessions, a touch of secrecy. I was all for being rebellious in those days. Maybe Old Nurse Reid felt the need to rebel also. How oldmustyou be before you can say with authority, "stuff convention!" Certainly, ancient enough to have earned the prefix, 'old'.

Here is a photo of me painting a big

portrait. I'm just putting it here randomly because I thought you might like to see me at work.

Having read or perhaps skipped through this

far you will be aware that I have recently joined a couple of online dating sites and I did promise to keep you updated on my progress. Or, as it turns out, lack of it.

There is in fact very little to tell you. I had one date with a very nice lady. That's it. One date. But that one date, pleasant as it was, convinced me that I really and truly enjoy my life the way that it is.

I should be honest with myself and freely admit that I am selfish and unwilling to change. Probably, as I am being brutal with myself, I should also admit that I would be unable to change anyway. Because, if I were to share my life, full time, with another, it would inevitably require some changes.

Although I am alone, I am not lonely. I have some very good friends. Indeed, I have built up quite a social life for myself lately. In fact, it can be too hectic at times for this old guy, and I have to step back and take a rest from it all.

I think what motivated me to join the dating sites was the lack of an, ahem, intimate side to my life. Hey! I'm getting on a bit, but I am not dead yet. There still courses, well, flows, oh alright then, dribbles, through my veins the blood of a passionate man.

However, if I'm not prepared to put the effort into a relationship I can hardly expect anyone else to. I will just have to soldier on, alone but happy. Until the miracle occurs which sends Miss Wonderful, the perfectly understanding woman into my life. I am not holding my breath.

My subscriptions to the dating sites have been cancelled. I have seen the light. I am free from the need to be constantly checking my email inbox. No one will be contacting me. I will no longer have to suffer the indignity of not being tall enough, or solvent enough, or hirsute enough. I no longer have to feel guilty because I do not particularly like eating out, or going to the theatre. The inside of my car can go back to looking like a dustbin, and smelling like a dog kennel. The iron can go back into the cupboard where it belongs, and I can go back to my happy crumpled self. I don't care anymore. Because I am what I am. Not what I want some improbably perfect woman to think I am.

This is the finished big portrait I was up a step-ladder painting a few pages ago. In case you don't recognise him; It is Prince.

I've been lying in the bath for the last couple

of hours. It's been very pleasant. I was having a nice read of a magazine, 'Private Eye'.

There was a little article in there about an artist who has started a small business sharpening pencils. It's true!

People send him their pencils and he sharpens them. His unique selling point is that he sharpens them in the old-fashioned way, using a knife.

Modern pencil sharpeners are a complete no no for him. Apparently, he is able to get the pencils to a really sharp point. So as not to get the point damaged in the post, he then puts the pencil in its own snug fitting tube. This service only costs $12. It sounds crazy but he is doing a roaring trade.

It seems that once sharpened people are reluctant to use them for the intended purpose, and instead give them as gifts to others. They come with a little certificate to prove they have been hand sharpened.

So, as I was lying there in the bath, my thoughts turned to rusty nails. Specifically, as to whether I would be able to make any money from them.

I have a great heap of rusty nails, mostly garnered from the embers of the occasional bonfire I have and also from burning wooden pallets and packing cases in the fire in the cold winter months. I suppose I ought to reclassify them as burnt rusty nails.

If I had a welding machine I could make little sculptures and sell them for lots of money to art collectors. That would take up a lot of my time though, and in the end, they might not even sell.

Because they have been in the fire they have lost their temper. No, I don't mean they are angry about being burnt. I mean they have gone a bit soft and bendy. Obviously, they are not going to be any use for their original purpose.

What I have decided to do, is to sell them individually, mounted on their own little wooden plaque. With a label stating that they have been burnt in a genuine Sussex bonfire. They can be supplied in original burnt and rusty condition, or polished, or a choice of three colours.

I'm going to charge £9.99p for them. My reasoning being, that people will notice that they cost less than a tenner and think that they are getting a bargain. Which of course they are. This money-making idea cannot fail. I shall probably become a millionaire.

Amazing that this has all stemmed from reading a magazine whilst sitting in the bath. Next time I'm going to put some water in the bath. It might relax me a bit. Stop me from being such a bloody idiot.

The first time I set eyes on him he was

involved in a tug of war with a pretty young veterinary nurse. She was losing the war and being a gallant young sailor with an eye for a pretty face it was only right that I should go to her assistance. He was a big German

Shepherd and extremely determined not to go through the door into the Vets surgery.

Between the pretty nurse and me we managed in the end through a combination of tugging, pushing and cajoling to get him halfway through the door, at which stage this big dog made a beeline for the examination table and cowered underneath it, panting, and wild eyed with what looked like total panic.

My eyes now prick with tears as I recall and relate this tale, because it turned out that the reason this magnificent animal was at the Vets in the first place was to be put down.

The pretty nurse told me what had happened. Just a short while before I came along, a man had left him there, instructed the Vet to put him to sleep, paid the euthanasia fee and quickly left. Luckily, she was holding tight to his lead because the dog had tried to run off. Maybe the big dog was panicking at the sudden loss of his owner, or perhaps he knew what he was there for. Whatever the reason it was heart-breaking to see him eyes wide and scrabbling with fright on the polished floor.

It is difficult to remember exactly how it happened, but a short while later, having let my heart rule my head, and after the Vet had given the dog a thorough examination, and found him to be in perfect health, I walked out from the surgery with a new friend. I think the Vet had already decided that he would not put the dog to sleep. I was there at the right time.

Danny Boy. 1967. My Magnificent Friend.

The year was 1967 or thereabouts. I was on my way to catch a bus to visit my Mother, having just disembarked from a ship in Aberdeen docks, and it was quite a struggle to get this giant chap to come along with me. It was more tugging and cajoling but eventually we reached the bus station and boarded the bus. Where the big fellow headed straight for the back and hid under a seat, still shaking with fear. He didn't like it when the bus began to move and started to whine nervously. I did my best to calm him, stroking and talking to him constantly, but I am sure from the amount of hard looks I got and the tutting of some of the other passengers they thought that the dog's nervousness was down to me.

After an hour, we got off the bus, much to mine, and I'm sure the dogs, relief. But there was still a walk of several miles to Mum's place. He was still reluctant to come with me though and there was more pulling and cajoling. Add to this the fact that I had a heavy kit bag on my shoulder and it made things very difficult.

There was a point in the walk where by crossing diagonally across a couple of fields it is possible to shorten the journey and avoid a dangerous bend in the road. I took this option and this is the place where a miraculous change in the dog's behaviour occurred.

We were off the road, the fields were clear of livestock, and I decided to let him off the lead. At first I thought that I had made a dreadful mistake, because he went haring off down the hill like a bat out of hell, and just as I thought I would never see him again, he turned and came haring back up the hill towards me. What a relief! Of course, I made a big fuss of him. He wanted to play. We ran down the hill together and at the bottom he plunged straight into a stream and ran splashing along it. He seemed to revel in his freedom. He was a different animal. I cannot explain this change in his behaviour, but this is not a made-up tale. It happened and he was transformed. From that happy moment on he was my dog.

Up until that moment I had it in mind to leave him with my Mother. I knew she would love him and he would give her a sense of security, living as she did on her own in the middle of nowhere.

It did turn out that way in the end, but not before my new friend, whom I named Danny Boy, and I had enjoyed an adventurous time together, tramping and wild camping, in the highlands of Scotland.

Danny was of a sweet, and gentle temperament. However, he had been highly trained and I sensed that he had abilities which I never got to find out about.

I can only imagine the reason why anyone would want to have him put down. Perhaps his real owner had died and nobody could take such a big animal on.

Whatever the reason, I am so pleased that I happened along that day to help a pretty veterinary nurse, and give Danny Boy a new lease of life.

The inbox was full up, so I decided to delete all

my emails. That was about an hour ago, I have just checked my emails again. There is nothing there. It's been an hour. No emails. Not even spam! Why did I delete everything? Now I know for certain that nobody loves me.

Maybe I have too much time on my hands? Too much time for introspection.

I am unwell. Have been for a couple of weeks. The Doctor has given me tablets. Sometimes I think they are working. Sometimes I think they are not. Right now as I sit here writing this, they are most definitely not. My head keeps spinning. Not literally! I am not an extra from the film 'The Exorcist'. Oh, dear oh dear! Why did I say that? Now I must look up how to spell exorcist. It doesn't look right to me.

I'm back! That is the correct spelling. Anyway, as I was saying. My head is spinning. The Doctor thinks it is a condition called 'labrinthitis'. An inner ear infection. I'm not convinced. I bet it is something far more serious. Besides, everyone I talk to has had labrinthitis. Which makes it far too run of the mill for me. Far too common. If I'm going to be ill I prefer something a little more exotic. But easily curable of course.

The word 'to' or 'too' is bothering me now. I am having trouble knowing which to use. Ah yes! That was the correct usage in the sentence before I said 'Ah yes'. Excuse me while I go back to the beginning of the second paragraph and change a couple of to's to too.

I have just changed two to's to too, which is not something a lot of people have to do, or say, very often. Another unique moment in my life.

Are you still there? That is so kind of you. I know I have been rambling on a bit.

I have just read the leaflet that came with the tablets. They are called prochlorperazine maleate. They are for treating dizziness or balance problems. One of their other uses, it says here, is to treat, over active behaviour or thoughts. Fortunately, that is not something that bothers me. They are also used to treat schizophrenia. Do you think the Doctor is keeping something from me? Maybe he is trying to tell me something. Well it's not working if he is.

Oh, my word! I have just had a read of the possible side effects of these pills. Scary stuff. Wish I hadn't looked.

Two hours. Still no emails. So, it must be true then. Nobody loves me. Hey! Wait a second. This isn't schizophrenia. This is paranoia. Hey! I'm on the wrong tablets. I had better get back to the Doctors. Wish my head would stop spinning, so I could determine which direction his surgery is in.

Perhaps I had better not write today. Yes, sorry no writing today. I'm not thinking straight. It would probably be a lot of rambling rubbish. You deserve better than that.

The good news is that George, my extremely handsome son has fully recovered from his knee injury and subsequent operation and has now been discharged by the physiotherapist.

College has finished for the summer holidays and he has decided to return to his part time job working in the forest.

In these days of rampant health and safety rules a pair of steel toe capped boots are a necessity. No boots, no work, is the mantra. George is a growing boy he needs new boots, and hereby hangs a tale.

Let us go back to Saturday last. George and his Mother Tricia, drove into the beautiful West Sussex cathedral city of Chichester. Their purpose was to buy a new pair of work boots for George.

If only they had told me they were going. I could have persuaded George to try the new boots on. He tends to listen to me. His Mothers entreaties on the other hand tend to be overlooked. I have no idea why, except that it is a boy thing. I was a boy once, but it was a long time ago, and I have forgotten why boys don't listen to their Mothers, if I ever knew.

The boots with which the intrepid duo returned home were, as boots go, quite beautiful. Black matt leather uppers with polished toecaps. The soles and heels were sturdily crafted from the finest rubber. Designed to deal with all kinds of situations. The uppers where they encased the ankle were softly padded. Blisters would not be a problem. Personally, I thought they were a bit overpriced, but I think everything is overpriced these days. All things considered though they were good boots. But in the end whether good or bad was academic. They were the wrong size.

Disappointing? Yes, but a situation such as this is easily rectified. Simply a case of returning to the shop and changing them for the correct size. But not today. Nobody feels inclined to take another trip to town. Remember it is Saturday, the traffic will have built up by now. Trying to park will be horrendous. It will have to wait now, until Monday. Which as it happened, turned out to be a good decision.

Look at the notice I saw in the local shop window when I happened past later that day. Brand new work boots. Still in their box. The right size. Best of all, only fifteen quid. An absolute bargain. Perfect!

Tricia was in such a hurry to go and buy these bargain boots, that as she rushed to get into her car she was inches away from colliding with a cyclist, who in trying to avoid her was almost knocked off his bike by a passing car. The driver of which told the cyclist what he thought of him in very unpleasant terms, at the same time as the cyclist was telling Tricia what he thought of her. Which was also uncomplimentary, and certainly no way to talk to a lady. Which Tricia is. Occasionally.

Unfortunately, another incident involving the same cyclist occurred further down the road, when as she was overtaking him, another car coming from the other direction, forced Tricia to cut in sharply, and without warning, across said cyclists path. Tricia does not lip read but she thinks from the expression on his face, as viewed in her rear-view window, that he may have been saying rude words to her. She didn't stop to find out. Or apologise. She wanted those boots.

She got them too, and they fitted my extremely handsome son George perfectly. So, all is well that ends well.

Except. As she returned home Tricia forgot to check before she opened the car door. Just at that moment a cyclist was passing by. He had to take swift avoiding action. Forcing a car coming the other way to brake sharply. The driver of which wound down his window and told the poor man exactly what he thought of bloody cyclists. It was the same hapless cyclist who had already had two unfortunate encounters with her. Apparently, his language on this occasion was even more appalling.

Tricia was quite ashen faced as she related these incidents to me. I dread to think what colour the poor cyclists face was. Or his trousers!

There had been a bit of an altercation at

the Saturday night dance. A bit of a ruckus. The occasional punch may have been thrown. The odd, so called 'Glesga' kiss', might have been bestowed. Usually the result of too much beer and whisky being taken. Oh! You know what I mean. Or you would do, if you had been to a Saturday night hop in the 1960's.

I was a stranger in this little town in Aberdeenshire, Scotland. Fortunately, I was not alone for long. My charismatic persona, handsome chiselled good looks, and flowing black hair, had, as always, attracted the girls. It was ever thus.

Perhaps one of the local lads had become jealous of my success with the local lasses and kicked off. I had this problem a lot in those days. It was something I had learned to live with.

Well anyway, a fight had started. There were only about twenty of the local lads against little me, so it was a foregone conclusion that they would come off worse. I mean come on, twenty small town youths against me, a nineteen-year-old merchant navy deckhand, who had fought in some of the roughest bars and dance halls known to man. What chance did they have?

The first plane I ever flew in was a de Havilland Comet. The world's first commercial jet liner. It was only a short flight, from London to Aberdeen in Scotland. I remember a slight trepidation as I boarded. The weather was awful. Blowing a gale and pouring with rain.

Somehow, we managed to take off and stay airborne. It
was a bit of a bumpy ride. I believe the captain referred to
it as slight turbulence. That however is not the description
I used at the time. We were also struck by lightning twice
as we descended towards Aberdeen. Apart from that it was
pretty uneventful. Even so I was relieved when we landed
safely, and I made a silent vow not to repeat the experience
if I could help it. I think the detective sergeant I was hand-
cuffed to at the time, was also quite pleased to be safely
back on terra firma.

Now if I'm any judge of character, you are probably sat
there, avidly devouring my words, wondering what I was
doing on an aircraft. Well, I am just about to tell you all
about it.

What's that? Oh, the hand-cuffs. The detective. Sorry I
nearly forgot. I'll tell you about that as well.

It had all started with the aforementioned dance hall fight. The local police had been round to see me the next day. There had been a complaint, - honestly some people! They were keen to hear my version of events. As it transpired, they were keen to put their version of events to me, and for me to confess that the whole thing was all my fault.

After they had left to frame a case against me, sorry, I meant to say, further their inquiries, I decided that it would be prudent on my part if I left town. I hitchhiked down south.

Which is how I came to be in London at the shipping federation offices, looking to sign on for a long voyage on the first available ship. Which is where I was, sat patiently on a bench in the outer office, when two officers of the Metropolitan police force arrived and arrested me for evading a summons. Which is how, dear reader I found myself hand-cuffed to a detective, being rocked and jolted violently by turbulence, in a de Havilland Comet jet liner on my way back to bonny Scotland to face the wrath of the Sheriffs court.

To tell the truth I got a bit of a kick out of the situation. I could see the other passengers looking at me and wondering just what sort of criminal I was. I bet some of them got a kind of vicarious thrill about being sat next to this violent bank robber, this international drug dealer, this notorious jewel thief. I was quite pleased that they did not realise I was only in this position for a lowly 'breach of the peace'.

There was a nice meal served on board. Because of the handcuffs, it was a bit difficult to eat. My detective escort made me promise that I would not attempt to escape if he removed the cuffs. I had to remind him that we were at thirty-five thousand feet and I did not have a parachute. He saw the humour and laughed at my joke. He was a nice guy actually, and I think he was as bemused as I was by the situation we found ourselves in. He had quickly and correctly decided that I was not a bad person.

There was hell to pay when I finally stood in the dock. Hell to pay! But not for me. Oh no! The Sheriff, Lord Hamilton, a judge whom I had been before frequently during my unhappy teens, unleashed his fury on the justice system, namely the police, who had wasted their time and everyone else's in bringing me back to Scotland. By air! From London! Ridiculous he said. The lad had not even received the summons. I agreed with his Lordship of course and sagely nodded my agreement, feeling extremely self-righteous. It was true I had left before the summons had arrived.

Of course, I plead not guilty, and my good friend the sheriff was of a mind to agree with me. Indeed, he even told the police to issue me with a rail warrant, so that I could fulfil my original intent and ship out on a voyage from London.

Justice. It is such a marvellous thing. Especially if, just for once, you are on the right side of it.

I've never been one to worry

about gaining weight but it has to be said, my waist measurement has slowly and remorselessly crept up over the years. This fact was recently brought home to me when I decided to buy a new suit.

When the salesperson, a thin, anaemic, spotty faced youth, enquired my waist size I told him, thirty-four inches. At which point he raised his eyebrows, appeared to smirk patronisingly, and reached for his tape measure.

"Sir has gained a few inches." He said smugly. He is very lucky that the shop was full of customers, because I wanted to punch him.

The first time I can recall my waist size meaning anything to me was when I was a snake hipped twenty-nine inches.

After I married it suddenly became thirty inches, probably because of having regular meals for the first time since childhood. Although I would have thought that being newly married, and forced against my will to indulge in lots of lovemaking, would have kept me slim. But it didn't. Perhaps my technique was wrong. Maybe I shouldn't have let her do all the work.

Being a lazy lover, sitting watching lots of television, and yes, I'll admit it, being spoilt by my wife, gradually added another two inches, and there it stayed for a good long while. That was all right though. I didn't mind it being thirty-two inches. I knew plenty of men my age who were a heck of a lot bigger round the middle.

Suddenly though, one day I found that a thirty-two-inch waistband seemed a little tight on me. How did that happen?

Maybe when my wife began to call me cuddly she was trying to point something out to me. Perhaps I was wrong to take her words as a compliment. Should I have taken her frequent references to my love handles as a warning? Could she have simply been trying to avoid the word fat?

You can't buy a pair of trousers with a thirty-three-inch waist. At least not off the peg. So, I had to have a thirty-four-inch size, which to be perfectly honest fitted nicely and were very comfortable to wear.

I wasn't happy with the extra inches though and silently promised myself that I would cut down on the cakes and biscuits which I blamed for the morbidly obese condition I found myself in. Thirty-four-inch waistline. Ugh! Disgusting!

My new resolution was short lived. Actually, it was never really born. The truth is it evaporated into thin air the very next time I smelt the aroma of freshly cooked doughnuts in the local shop. Which time lapse was about two hours. I have always been a man of steely resolve. Still not to worry though. These resolutions always take a little time to really get going. Besides thirty-four inches is not so bad, is it? The trouble is though, that if you feel comfortable in your larger trousers, it is easy to forget why they were necessary in the first place.

I am shocked and saddened to have to tell you that this, my latest attempt at trouser buying has left me mortified. A thirty-four-inch waist will no longer suffice. The smug salesman was right. The skinny, condescending little bastard!

I hold my head in my hands. I sob, albeit in a discreet, and manly way.

My waist. No! The word waist is a falsehood. It is no longer a waist. My girth. There I've said it. My big fat girth measures thirty-six inches. Thirty-six inches! That's a metric yard. Blimey! Never mind a yard, that is big enough to be a backyard! A girth is also the name of the strap which holds a horse's saddle on. It goes all the way around the horse's middle. That says it all really. I am a fat man.

If that is my waist size how big must my backside appear. No! I'm not going to look. It will be far too upsetting. It must be horrendous.

It is not entirely my fault though. The disappearance of my waist is due to me having big genes. Or should that be big jeans. Never been too sure how to spell that word.

Perhaps I should have taken more notice when I realised that I no longer felt comfortable in medium size underpants, and was having to buy the large size. Oh, the ignominy of it. I had put it down to the Chinese, who seem to have cornered the market in these articles, being quite small people.

Thank goodness for supermarkets. At least they make it possible to buy big underpants without having to ask for them by name.

I will not be trying to solve the problem by wearing tracksuit bottoms, or trousers with an elasticated waistband. No way. I have seen men who have adopted this solution, and they look like they have given up the battle of the bulge. They look like losers. Not losers of weight. That is not for me. I am going to fight like a man. Oh, dear God! Now I have just had a vision of a fat man fighting. It is not pleasant. I have no intention of gaining the proportions of a sumo wrestler.

What a weak willed, burger scoffing, cake munching fool I've been. Not much wonder I can't find a girlfriend. Women must run a mile when they see me waddling towards them.

Oh well. Nothing else for it. I shall starve myself for a couple of weeks. Soon be back to my skinny self. After which, with my track record, I shall probably begin to lose the fat fight all over again.

What a good thing I'm not one to worry about gaining weight.

It is 1959. I am twelve years old, and have been in Scotland for less than a day, having spent my life so far in a children's home and with various foster parents, in London, England. My Mother, who is a virtual stranger to me, has brought me to her new home, a small croft of seven acres in the quiet Aberdeenshire countryside. She has just remarried, and her new husband Jimmy is due home from his work at any minute.

I am feeling nervous about meeting him for the first time. Mum tells me he is a 'fine manny' and reassuring as that sounds, I think I will wait and make up my own mind. I have met quite a few 'fine men' in my few short years on planet earth.

We shake hands politely Jimmy and I, as Mum looks on, smiling in the proud way Mothers do.

He is smiling too and I notice that he has extremely white teeth. Obviously false, and a little bit loose. There is an enormous jagged scar down one side of his face, stretching from his temple to his chin. On his rather large head is a flat cap, which in those days all men of a certain age wore on weekdays and Saturdays. I can't say for certain but I suspect that quite a few men also wore them in bed. On

Sundays, and for funerals trilby's would be worn. There is evidence of a short back and sides haircut under his cap. Beneath his faded navy blue boiler suit is a white shirt and a tie. In those days, even a lowly labourer would wear a shirt and tie when working. It was not unusual to see a road mender wearing a suit either. Jimmy is not a tall man, but he is well built and looks tough and powerful, and I already know from Mum that he was once a good amateur wrestler. The hand that grips mine firmly is strong and hard, a product of his work in the local granite quarry.

"Fit like Loon," he says. "are ye fair waabit? Hiv ye heen a fly an a piece?"

I don't have a clue what he has just said and stare at him blankly, transfixed by his loose teeth, and strange language.

"He disnae ken fit your saying Jimmy," says Mum in her soft highland brogue, and they both look at me and laugh.

Jimmy tries again,"how are you?" He asks, speaking slowly and deliberately, in what he probably imagines to be an English accent, "are you tired? Are you hungry?"

"I'm alright thank you," I say, in what I think is perfect English.

"awright fank you,"mimics Jimmy in a poor attempt at a cockney accent. Mum joins in with his laughter. It is apparent that he and I might have some communication problems. He seems nice enough though. At least he has a sense of humour.

"Tell Jimmy what you've been practicing," says Mum, adding, as she notes my nervousness, "he's been practicing specially for you Jimmy. Go on John."

I am embarrassed, "do I have to?"

"Yes. Come on you can do it."

I take a deep breath, "It's a braw brecht meen licht nicht the nicht."

"Aye nae bad," says my new Dad, "nae bad a va."

As far as I'm concerned, he might as well be speaking a foreign language. Mum explains, "he's impressed,"

Oh dear! I have an awful lot of learning to do.

manny: man

Fit like Loon: how are you boy

fair waabit: very tired

have ye heen a fly and a piece: have you had a drink and something to eat

disnae ken: doesn't understand

braw brecht meen licht nicht the nicht: nice moonlight night tonight

aye nae bad nae bad a va: yes not bad at all

I bought this old scythe at a car boot sale. The blade is in a terrible state and I have decided that it is not worth the effort of restoring it. But I am going to use it today to illustrate why it is important to pay heed to warnings about sharp implements.

Here comes another anecdote from my time with my stepfather Jimmy.

Come haymaking time and several of Jimmy's friends would turn up at the croft with their scythes, ready for a day's work. They did not get paid for their labour. It was a common reciprocal thing in this area of Scotland. At haymaking or harvest time all the neighbours would help each other out. In those days before the ordinary man could afford machinery to do the work it was a good thing to stay on friendly terms with other local crofters and farmers.

Have you ever watched an expert working with a scythe? They make it look so easy, and even enjoyable, as the cut their way through the long grasses. But it is not easy. It takes a long time to become proficient at mowing a meadow with a scythe.

I was keen to have a go, but I was not allowed. Not because I might injure myself. Oh no. But because I might injure the scythe. More precisely, I might damage the blade. Jimmy treated his scythe with a reverence normally associated with religious icons. Indeed, the whole business of looking after the scythe took on an air of ceremony. It had its own special place in one of the outbuildings. Where it was hung from its very own hook. It was cleaned and the blade sharpened, before being oiled and wrapped in hessian. Which hessian was also soaked in oil. When taken down for use it would have the oil carefully wiped from the blade and then sharpened again. All through the working day it would be regularly honed, so that it was always working at peak efficiency. It would be fair to say that Jimmy was very fond of his scythe.

It was fascinating to watch how he used the sharpening stone on the blade. This too was a great skill. His stubby hand holding the stone seemed to move at lightning speed over the whole length of the blade. It was without exaggeration, razor sharp. It fact it was sharper than a razor. He showed me how by lightly touching it with his thumbnail, he could send a ripple along the sharpened edge.

I was expressly forbidden from going anywhere near his scythe when he was not around, but I was mesmerised by it. It became an obsession with me. I wanted to have a go a scything the grass, but most of all I wanted to have a go at sharpening the blade, with the stone, the way that Jimmy

did. It surely wouldn't hurt to have a go. It looked so easy.
I waited my chance, till one day when Jimmy was at work
and my Mother was busy indoors.

Mum became hysterical when she saw all the blood, and
all she could do was scream and throw a towel at me. I was
in a bit of a state myself, but wrapped the towel around my
hand and ran down to the nearby farmhouse. Mrs Gilbert
the farmer's wife, had a stronger constitution than my
Mum. I had cut my thumb and forefinger through to the
bone. She cleaned the wound and staunched the flow of
blood as best she could, before pouring on a good splash of
whisky, and bandaging my hand tightly.

After a nice cup of hot sweet tea, the usual panacea in
those days. I was able to clean up the scythe and put it
back on its special hook.

If Jimmy noticed anything amiss he never mentioned it. I
just had to make sure he didn't see my bandaged hand for a
few days.

Do you know, I never even felt the blade cut me, it was so
sharp. If I hadn't looked down when I did I might easily
have sliced my fingers clean off.

The scars are a constant reminder that I was young once,
and thought I knew it all.

The even mead that erst brought sweetly forth

The freckled cowslip, burnet and green clover

Wanting the scythe, all uncorrected,rank

Conceives by idleness, and nothing teems

But hateful docks, rough thistles, keksie, burs,

Losing both beauty and utility.

Shakespeare, Henry V

The term 'fishwife' is, or was, often

used in a derogatory manner. Mostly entirely wrongly in my view. These were hard working women, of great character, struggling to earn enough to supplement their fisherman husbands uncertain pay.

In its worse sense 'fishwife' was used to describe a woman of dubious moral standards. In that respect, and though it pains me to say it, my Mother would probably qualify at times, although there were some nicer aspects to her character, which made people like her. At least initially.

When she was good, as they say, she was very, very good, but when she was bad, she was horrid. Barbara on the other hand most definitely did not qualify. I loved her.

A short woman of large proportions, she was nearly as wide as she was tall. What a face she had. Open, smiling and pleasant to look at. Full of joy. Full of contentment. Full of hope. Full of love.

Love for Bob, her trawlerman husband. Love for her three beautiful teenage daughters, Elsie, Alice, and Jean. Love for her friends. Love for her friend's children.

Things were beginning to go wrong at home between my Mum and Jimmy her new husband, and I would often be sent to stay with 'Auntie Barbara' at her home in Aberdeen.

She and her daughters would spoil me rotten. Barbara and I and her border collie, Lassie, would often get up early and go for coach trips to Braemar. I think it was on these days out that I would develop my love for the mountains.

Of course, I loved all the attention. Especially from the girls. At twelve or thirteen I was rapidly developing an interest in the fairer sex. Not that I let them know it of course, they were older than me. Besides which, I was far too shy.

I was in seventh heaven, when Barbara and the girls would sit in company with me, playing board games or cards. Alice, who just edged it, as my favourite, with her long red hair, would give me lessons on the piano. My word it was hard to concentrate, with her sitting so close against me on the piano stool. Especially when she had to lean across me, to show which key to hit, or to turn a page of the music.

Bob was often at sea, but when he was home I would watch Barbara and the girls fuss around him. It made me realise how good family life could be. There were no arguments or fights in their house, at least not that I could see. Occasionally I would see one or the other of the girls looking sad, but that was because of boyfriend trouble usually. These lovely girls were not without an interested suitor for long though.

Elsie, the eldest daughter was always wanting to take me shopping for new clothes. Perhaps I was a scruffy kid. I'm certainly a scruffy man.

One day, lovely Elsie spent almost a whole month's wages on buying me a suit. She just did it out of pure kindness. Truly a daughter that Barbara and Bob could be proud of. Despite my unhappy childhood, I think it was remembering times such as this, that ultimately saved me from going even further down the wrong path, than I did.

Where money was concerned, my stepfather Jimmy was, what would kindly be called 'careful'. Money was probably what he and Mum argued about most.

I think Barbara and the girls felt sorry for my Mum, and thought she deserved some help. Buying things for me was one way they could help ease her financial woes.

Jimmy wasn't poor. In fact, due to his 'careful' nature, he was quite wealthy. The trouble was, that after a lifetime of struggling along on very little, Mum was profligate with cash, and after the brief honeymoon period, Jimmy had tightened the purse strings.

There were other reasons why they argued almost constantly. These reasons will become apparent as my story unfolds. They are for another day.

One day Bob did not come home. He had died of a heart attack at sea. Barbara was devastated by the loss of her childhood sweetheart, and she too had a fatal heart attack a few months later. But to my mind she simply could not adjust to life without him, and succumbed to a broken heart.

The girls all married and went their separate ways. Mum and Jimmy argued on. I ended up back in 'care', in a children's home.

The circle of sadness and longing for a normal life had briefly broken. I had experienced happiness. Now the ragged ends had met again.

Last night I went to an open mic night for the

first time in three weeks. The thing is, they, the ladies that is, have been missing me. Pining actually. I felt that it would be wrong to deprive them any longer. So, even though I am having difficulty staying erect, hey stop that! I mean upright. Oh dear! Just as bad. Anyway, I fall over a lot at the moment. No, it has nothing to do with alcohol, it's because of this labrynthitis thing. Anyway, I went along and sang a few sexy love songs for them.

They all went home happy at the end of the evening, so obviously, my charms are still working. The husbands were happy too, pleased that I had got their wives in the mood for love. They all thought they were on a promise. I like to think that I am doing my bit for mankind. Helping my species to survive. I am truly altruistic.

So, it was a late night. It was also an early morning. I had to be up early so that I could go to the house and wake my extremely handsome Son George up for work. His Mum was away overnight and thought he wouldn't get up in time, so I was designated. He was up and about when I got there. Oh, ye of little faith. He loves working in the woods. Of course, he was up. I have no idea why I'm telling you this bit. Rambling again.

The dizzy spells came back with a vengeance today, just as I was trying to solve my television reception problems. My thought was that the aerial needed to be higher. So, I have tied the existing pole to a long hazel branch, which in turn is tied to a post which is in turn nailed to the shed. As erections go it is not very strong. Hey! Stop that. But it is very high now, about thirty feet, and my reception is better. Of course, it will probably snap off next time the wind blows. Unfortunately, all that difficulty in getting it up. Hey! Stop that. Keeping it up. Hey! Stop that. Looking up, and pole balancing made me very dizzy indeed. Feeling a bit worried, I made an emergency appointment with the Doctor.

After chatting with him for a while, he managed to convince me that I am not going to have a heart attack. He thinks that I might have been standing too close to the loudspeakers at the open mic night. He thinks this, because

I told him that is what I did. Self-diagnosis really. It's just a theory I came up with, because I have been standing too close to the loudspeakers.

He now thinks that there is a piece of loose debris in my ear. Not half a brick or anything like that. Just bodily detritus which we all have apparently. Oddly enough, bizarrely even, he has referred me to a physiotherapist. She is going to jerk my head about to dislodge the debris. I'm not making this up! It is a tried and tested method which has good results.

Someone has to come with me to ensure I get home safely. It seems that all the head shaking can leave you feeling a bit disorientated. Ha! Never did me any harm in my punk rocker days. I always managed to get home then. Oh really, what am I saying?

He also gave me some more tablets. They're a bit stronger than the last ones. I see the physio next week. Should be interesting.

Despite my spinning head, I managed to mow the paddock when I got home. Yes, I know it was silly, but it needed doing badly. No, not badly. It needed doing goodly. Oh, blast it, let's just say it needed doing. It looks much nicer with the grass cut.

I took one of the new stronger tablets at 3 o'clock. I woke up in my armchair at 7 o'clock. Four hours zonked out, and very dizzy. I won't be taking any more of those!

That's the story of my last twenty-four hours. I couldn't get my head cleared enough to think what else to write about, and I hate letting you down.

Especially the ladies.

It was two years ago, that I had to

make the decision that the two Gloucester old spot pigs, Bluebell and Snowdrop had to go. It wasn't an easy decision, and I was worried what George would think about it, because it was his idea to have them in the first place.

I must admit that the idea appealed to me too. I had seen pictures of Gloucester old spots. They looked so happy, living an idyllic life in their little orchard.

I forgot that I don't have an orchard. Not for the first time where animals are concerned I allowed my heart to rule my head.

The thing is they didn't remain as cute little piggy wiggies for long. They grew enormous in a very short space of time.

They were free ranging, and this plot of mine was beginning to look like a battle field. They just love to dig.

They looked so sweet and innocent when they first arrived.

When it rained, they churned the place up so much that a lot of the time they were knee deep in mud. I know pigs are supposed to like mud, but I was worried about their welfare.

We made them an area of hard standing and confined them to it when it got really wet, but it didn't seem right to keep them confined. They had to go.

When we first got them, the intention was that they would be slaughtered when they had reached the appropriate size. I know how nice free range pork tastes, and looked forward to being self-sufficient in meat.

Really it is not a good idea to give a name to any animals which are destined for the table. It is not a good idea to take them for walks. It is not a good idea to bath them. It is not a good idea to tickle their tummies. It is not a good idea to introduce them to visitors who say, "aaah". It is not a good idea to start thinking of them as family pets.

Even though when we first acquired them, it was on the strict understanding that eventually they would have to go for slaughter, somehow, when I mentioned it was time, the rules were suddenly different.

Apparently, what I had agreed to was that Bluebell and Snowdrop would be brought to the boar, and that the resulting litters would then be sold for meat. I cannot recall saying this but it seems I am quite forgetful at times.

So, they stayed for about four years causing havoc. Luckily, I was able to avoid them meeting with the boar. The thought of lots more little piggy's adding to the battleground was too much to even contemplate.

Eventually though my commonsense prevailed, and George and his Mum saw that I just did not have enough space, or money, to keep them. Yes success!

No not really. I had to agree that Bluebell and Snowdrop would not be killed, and that I would find them a home where the new owner would not kill them either. In other words, I had to find them a home where they would be able to live out their lives in free ranging happiness.

Who is going to agree to give a home for life to two of the biggest pigs you ever saw? Who is going to be that daft?

Well, there was someone, and Bluebell and Snowdrop are happily ensconced in their new home on a small holding not too far away.

They have both had litters. It is wonderful to see them so happy. It is wonderful to know that they are not on my plot.

Do you know what? I am ever so glad that I never got to eat them. I am ever so glad that I am what is commonly known around here as 'an old softie'.

The last couple of days have been

horrible. Sniff. I have had the worst case of man flu to ever not be documented. Cough, splutter.

Today I feel a little bit better, but please, that is not an excuse for you to not feel very sorry for me. There might yet be a relapse. Also, don't forget that I have been suffering, and I don't use the word suffering lightly, or very often, I have been suffering, suffering I say, from extreme head spinning. Sniff, cough. Not literally of course. That would be fatal. Achoo! Excuse me.

I've had to cancel my appointment with the head jerking, dizziness removing, physiotherapist. It's just one thing after another. Sniff. So, I'll have to keep spinning away until the man flu has gone.

If you were to combine just a few of my symptoms, sniff, including, the running nose, the sneezing, the coughing, the excruciatingly painful sore throat, the current headache, the iron band squeezing my skull, cough, the popping in my ears causing recurrent deafness, - although strangely enough I can still hear the popping - the loss of appetite, excuse me, while I blow my nose, the tendency towards extreme grumpiness, and the hot one minute, cold the next fever, you would realise that this is not just a common or garden head cold, as some unfeeling people have suggested. You would also realise what a martyr I am being, sniff, cough, splutter, in calling by here to write this blog post.

Mind you, those are just some of my symptoms. There are others which I have tried to look up on the internet. Without success. It would seem that I am a bit of a medical phenomenon.

Some people have suggested that it is a miracle I am still alive. Some have suggested that I re-write my will, and leave my body to medical science. Although quick to add, that any monies I may have left to them. Achoo! Excuse me. Should not be interfered with, unless to increase it. They have got some hope. There is no way that I will be wasting the back of another envelope.

It is at times like this that I begin to wonder if living alone is a good thing or not. Sniff. There is no one here to answer my call for a hot whisky toddy. Splutter, cough. Or to bring me a cold flannel to ease my aching head. Cough. No one here to tell me what a brave boy I am being. Not that the last one is really necessary, I already know how brave I am. Sniff. But you know what I mean, we all need someone with us when we feel poorly. If only to pass on whatever it is we have got.

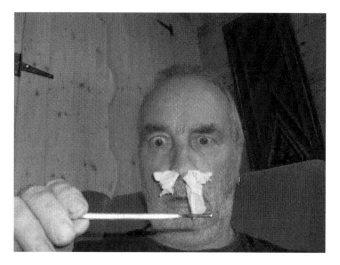

This man flu has even caused me to have a double chin!

Not that I would want anyone to have this what I have. Which is bad, very bad, as you may have gathered. Sniff, cough. Not that I am the kind of person to make a fuss about things. Cough. Even though it is terrible. Sniff.

Just leave me! Go! Let me do my suffering in silence, and let me tell you I don't use the word suffering lightly, or very often. Cough.

No! I'm sorry. Don't go. Please. I didn't mean to be nasty. It's the illness. It makes me grumpy. Are you still there? I need a hug. Splutter, sniff, cough, sob!

I just had a thought. Cough. Suppose it's swine flu. My last post was about pigs. Can you contract swine flu just by writing about pigs? What if some enormous coincidence has taken place? I'm going to check out the symptoms. Sniff.

I couldn't get through on the swine flu helpline, all I got was crackling!

Anyway, enough about my problems. Cough. How are you? I hope you are well. Sniff. I just thought I'd drop by and cheer you up. Cough. In case you were feeling a bit down. Mind you, I expect you were fine before you read this. Splutter.

Did I mention my bad back? Achoo! Please excuse me.

This hideously decayed, run down,

leaky roofed, holes in the floor, former holiday mobile home is my 'studio'. I call it my 'studio' because it is the place where I paint my masterpieces, and because I am a pretentious old fool who suffers from delusions of grandeur.

It is a good idea to have a 'studio' if you are a painter, so that when people ask you if you have your own 'studio', you can say with complete honesty as you hand them a gold edged card, with the words 'The John Bain Studio' embossed upon it, "oh yes, absolutely".

Of course, if as an artist, you have a propensity towards pretension, the fact of having your own 'studio' is an absolute must. Even if it looks like this one of mine.

What you must not do under any circumstances, especially the circumstance that your 'studio' looks like this one, is allow anyone, other than your closest friends, to visit your 'studio'. The artist whilst knowing the value of a 'studio' should also understand people can smell bullshit from a long distance. He, or she, must therefore have a ready list of excuses as to why the 'studio' is not available for visits.

My favourite all time excuse is the good old, "it's being redecorated at the moment". This excuse is also good when used in conjunction with the highly pretentious word, 'refurbishment'. It is important to use the word 'redecorated'. This plants in the mind of the potential visitor, the seed that the 'studio' must once have been decorated. This too adds to the sense that you do indeed have a very nice studio. Therefore, you must be a proper artist, which is why you charge such high prices.

Another acceptable excuse, particularly useful in the colder months is, "the heating has broken down". I do not let the fact that there is no heating to breakdown, deflect me from using it as an excuse. After all I might one day have heating installed, which might break down.

It is though, a bit of a pain that I have to lug all my equipment with me, in the event that I am required to paint a portrait from life. So, I have decided that I will build another, nicer, more salubrious 'studio'. One which I will be able to be properly pretentious about. One that I can invite visitors to. One that does not require the use of quotation marks whenever I mention the word.

There are problems involved however. In order that the new studio can be built, the old 'studio' must be demolished. In order that the demolition can take place it must first be emptied of stuff. In order that the cleared stuff has somewhere to be stored, the old shed, which is also full of 'stuff' must be cleared.

Problem number one, or is it number four, I have lost count, would appear to be, where can I put all the stuff from the old shed? Happily, the answer to this is close at hand, because right next to the old shed is a stable. The stable is a bit decrepit, but with some attention, it should be good enough to store the stuff from the old shed. I can't put my stuff from the 'studio' straight into the stable because it is not dry enough for my paintings and sundry art materials. The stuff from the stable will have to be stored outside under a tarpaulin in the meantime. Right! Good! O.K! Sorted! With a bit of luck, and a fair wind, I reckon I should be able to begin demolition work in a couple of years' time.

My 'studio' has been described as, "untidy". It has been described as "interesting". Friends have looked inside and described me as "a typical artist". At least I think that's what they said, but people do tend to mumble a bit when they see it. I am sure they are being kind.

I tend to think of my 'studio' as, "a bloody awful mess, which I shall tidy up tomorrow".

Which leads me to the main problem I have encountered. I just don't know where to start!

Perhaps I'll leave things as they are for now. Maybe a lick of paint might improve things.

If anyone wants to visit, that's no problem. I'm sure I'll be able to come up with an excuse as to why they can't.

Usually when a woman asks me to lie down on her couch, I think to myself, "aye, aye, Johnny boy, looks like your charms have worked the old magic again".

Not that I will allow situations like this to happen too frequently these days. I have to hold myself back a lot of the time from intimate encounters.

Women do tend to find me irresistible, and do throw themselves at me with a reckless abandon, which to be honest, at my age I can find a bit intimidating. So, the truth is, I tend these days to limit the amount of physical contact I allow myself to have with the opposite sex. I feel it is the decent, and kindest to thing to do. So many of the fairer sex have been disappointed in the past.

When I say, they have been disappointed, I am of course not referring to my abilities as a lover. That, it goes without saying really, has never been a problem for the lucky ones involved. No, what I mean is, that I just cannot spread myself thinly enough to accommodate all the ladies who want me. Oh dear, it is just so sad that there is only one of me, so unfair. I suppose that is the reason so many women just have to settle for second best.

Today though the couch in question belonged to the physiotherapist, and although she was an attractive lady, and I could immediately sense her interest in me, I thought it best to keep things on a professional level.

She began by asking me really personal questions, like, how many pillows do I have on my bed? Do I sleep well? Do I sleep on my right or my left side? Do I smoke? Do I drink? Things like that. There were so many questions that I can't remember most of them.

Then she got me to lay on my back on the couch and pushed my head through a hole. She said it was because she wanted to stretch my neck. That is not the first time someone has said that to me. Anyway, when she did that I got extremely dizzy and began to whine like a baby, "I want to sit up," I cried. But she then showed her mean side, and pushed my head down even further. Oh, it was horrible!

"I don't like you anymore," I sobbed, when finally, she relented. But then she suddenly twisted my head to one side, and told me to keep my nose pressed against the couch. She made sure that I obeyed by pushing down on my head with both hands. Just to compound things further she did the same on the other side.

When she eventually let me sit up, she had the cheek to ask me how I felt.

"Awful," I cried,wiping my eyes with a tissue. "That's the first and last time I allow myself to be manipulated by a woman."

She looked at me through eyes that I could not help noticing, were very beautiful. "Really?" she said.

"Hurry you two, if you want to see this." I
was excited as I cried out to them. They both turned to look at me.

"What's up, what's happening?" Called back my friend, who's name I don't know.

"It's frogs," I answered, "lots of them, quickly you two."

The older of the two men shouted back something but I didn't hear what he said, because he was hammering the wheel back onto the railway wagon, and I still had my wax ear plugs in.

"Hurry up," I urged, "or they'll all be gone."

My friend who's name I didn't know, never had known but I was certain he was interested in frogs, eventually came sauntering up.

"Where are they?" He sounded bored.

"Just over there on that barrel. Hundreds of them. What about the old bloke, doesn't he want to see them?"

"No, he's seen a frog before."

We ran over to the barrel. I was sad to see that most of the frogs had gone, and there were only three or four left. I felt a bit embarrassed, "sorry about this. There's not many left."

He pointed to a big frog, "that is not a frog," he stated emphatically. "That my friend is a lizard. Can't you see it's long tail?"

I did take a good look, and I had to agree with him. It was a lizard. It must have been hiding among all the frogs.

"Not only is it a lizard," he went on, "but it is a deadly venomous lizard. One bite from that, and you my friend, are dead."

Quickly I took out of my pocket a brown paper bag, and attempted to coax the lizard into it.

"That won't work," he said scornfully, "that lizard will be out of there in two seconds flat."

Just as he said it the lizard dashed into the bag, thrashed about madly, dashed out again, and threw itself off the barrel top, and onto the ground.

Amazingly the lizard changed into a beautiful woman before my very eyes. I was certain that I knew her from somewhere. "Excuse me Miss," I said, "but don't I know you from somewhere?"

She smiled at me. "Do you still want to take me to the cinema?"

Even though I knew that she might turn back into a poisonous lizard at any moment, I realised that I should not miss this opportunity to date such a truly beautiful woman.

Somehow in the excitement of the moment she and I got separated in the cinema. By the time, she found me again I was well and truly stuck in an extremely narrow stairwell. She rushed to get help.

The attendant who came to my aid was very kind, and wore a peaked cap. He brought me a cup of tea and a chocolate marshmallow biscuit, my favourite, whilst he went in search of a screwdriver. Unfortunately, he left the tea and biscuit just out of my reach.

Due to the stress I was under, my desire to drink the tea became a matter of life and death. I was desperate. As I struggled to reach them I was lucky enough to free myself, and shot out of the narrow stairwell like a cork from a bottle.

I woke up on the floor with the duvet wrapped tight around me.

In a hopeless attempt to shut out the

noise, I bury myself in my bed, a pillow over my head, under a thick pile of blankets, and cuddle up to Scamp, the little dog. He can't stand the shouting either, and his scrawny little body shakes uncontrollably as I hold him tight against me.

They are in the midst of yet another full volume argument, my Mother and stepdad Jimmy, and as usual I don't know how to deal with it and just want it to stop. At times like these I am full of trepidation. I should be on Mums side. I should go downstairs and look after her. But I sense that she is the main protagonist. Why can't they just be happy?

Not doing anything to help makes me feel useless and ashamed. But what can I do? I am thirteen years old. There is not a lot of me. My personal confidence level is at rock bottom. The brash, cocksure personality I attempt to exude, is a pathetic charade, a pretence, adopted to fool my new school friends into thinking I am a tough city kid not to be messed with.

The reality is, that I suffer from an inferiority complex, brought on by being abandoned to a life in children's homes under local authority care, by my feckless Mother. Abandoned more than once too. It is a complex brought on by being given hope so many times and then to have it snatched away, again and again. Situations like this must have an adverse effect on a growing boy. Of course, some of these feelings I would not have been able to put into words as a child, but they were there nevertheless. Planted by unthinking, or unfeeling parents.

They are arguing about the usual things tonight. Mainly to do with money and what Mum sees as Jimmy's meanness, but when my name is mentioned it naturally focuses my attention.

It seems that Jimmy wasn't told by my Mother, when he married her, that I was part of the deal. Jimmy had been expecting me to return to London after the summer holidays. He does not want the responsibility of having me there permanently. If I have to leave, Mum says that she will go too. Jimmy tells her to go then. It is a seemingly never ending round of accusation and counter accusation. Conducted at full and frightening volume. In my mind, the whole sorry situation is all my fault.

Eventually, emotionally exhausted, and fearful of what the morning has in store for me I fall into a fitful sleep, my face pressed into the softness of Scamps neck.

The short-lived normality, the happiness, the security of a home, of being with my Mother is about to be snatched away.

The next day, the council welfare officer comes to collect me. My Mother has done what she has always done when she feels she can't cope. Put me back into care. Another children's home. But I must not be too concerned I am told. It is only temporary. I will go back home when things settle down a bit.

Thinking back on it now, it occurs to me yet again, that in those days, a child's feelings were always a secondary consideration.

This time though, the raging hormones of puberty are upon me. Combine this with my ever-growing anger at life in general, and it is no wonder that I am about to go off the rails big time.

I really miss Scamp.

Here is another random photo. This one is
my new GermanShepherd Mia and me. Well, not that new
she has lived with me for three years now. She came to
live w ... old. Time flies.

There has been a slight concern in my
mind, that my extremely handsome son George, might be
shorter than me, once he attains adulthood. I cannot
explain why I have had this concern. It certainly has never
bothered him that he is usually the shortest lad among his

mates. In fact, he believes that being short in stature is a positive thing, particularly in the gym and on the football pitch.

Lately I have noticed that he seems to be catching up height wise with some of his friends, and perhaps he is no longer the shortest. This pleases me.

We were walking together along the pavement today, my extremely handsome son George and I, when he suddenly put his arm across my shoulder, and hugged me to him. Nothing unusual in this, he is a very loving boy. Takes after his dad in that respect. But do you know what he said, as he hugged me? He said:

"How are you doing little man?"

Yep, today my boy is taller than his dad. I'm pleased about that.

This is the end of my book. If it

becomes a best seller due to its amazing literary merit I might do another one. Thanks for reading it.

Printed in Great Britain
by Amazon